Hugh Kelly

The School for Wives

A Comedy

Hugh Kelly

The School for Wives
A Comedy

ISBN/EAN: 9783337038939

Printed in Europe, USA, Canada, Australia, Japan

Cover: Foto ©ninafisch / pixelio.de

More available books at **www.hansebooks.com**

School for Wives.

A COMEDY.

AS IT IS PERFORMED AT THE

THEATRE-ROYAL

IN

DRURY-LANE.

LONDON:

PRINTED FOR T. BECKET, IN THE STRAND. 1774.

[PRICE ONE SHILLING AND SIX-PENCE.]

PREFACE.

THE Author of the following performance cannot commit it to the press, without acknowledging the deepest sense of gratitude, for the uncommon marks of approbation with which he has been honoured by the Public.

Tho' he has chosen a title us'd by MOLIERE, he has neither borrowed a single circumstance from that great poet, nor to the best of his recollection from any other writer.—His chief study has been to steer between the extremes of sentimental gloom, and the excesses of uninteresting levity; he has some laugh, yet he hopes he has also some lesson; and fashionable as it has been lately for the wits, even with his friend Mr. Garrick at their head, to ridicule the Comic Muse, when a little grave, he must think that she degenerates into farce, where the grand business of instruction is neglected, and consider it as a heresy in criticism, to say that one of the most arduous tasks within the reach of literature, shou'd, when executed, be wholly without utility.

The Author having been presumptuous enough to assert, that he has not purloin'd a single sprig of bays from the brow of any other writer, he may perhaps, be ask'd, if there are not several plays in the English language, which, before his, produced Generals, Lawyers, Irishmen, Duels, Masquerades, and Mistakes? He answers, yes; and confesses moreover, that all the Comedies before his, were compos'd not only of men and women, but that before his, the great business of comedy consisted in making difficulties for the purpose of removing them; in distressing poor young lovers; and in rendering a happy marriage the object of every catastrophe.

Yet tho' the Author of the School for Wives, pleads guilty to all these charges, still, in extenuation of his offence, he begs leave to observe, that having

only

PREFACE.

only men and women to introduce upon the stage, he was oblig'd to compose his Dramatis Personæ of mere flesh and blood; if, however, he has thrown this flesh and this blood, into *new* situations; if he has given a *new* fable, and plac'd his characters in a point of light hitherto unexhibited:—he flatters himself that he may call his play, a *new* play, and tho' it did not exist before the creation of the world, like the famous Welch pedigree, that he may have some small pretensions to originality.

Two things besides the general moral inculcated thro' his piece, the Author has attempted; the first, to rescue the law, as a profession, from ridicule or obliquy; and the second, to remove the imputation of a barbarous ferocity, which dramatic writers, even meaning to compliment the Irish nation, have connected with their Idea of that gallant people:—The law, like every other profession, may have members who occasionally disgrace it; but to the glory of the British name, it is well know that in the worst of times, it has produced numbers whose virtues reflected honour upon human nature; many of the noblest privileges the constitution has to boast of, were derived from the integrity, or the wisdom of lawyers:

Yet

Yet the stage has hitherto cast an indiscriminate stigma upon the whole body, and laboured to make that profession either odious or contemptible in the theatre, which, if the laws are indeed dear to good Englishmen, can never be too much respected in this kingdom. There is scarcely a play in which a lawyer is introduced, that is not a libel upon the long robe; and so ignorant have many dramatic writers been, that they have made no distinction whatever, between the characters of the first Barristers in Westminster-Hall, and the meanest solicitors at the Old Bailey.

With respect to the gentlemen of Ireland, where even an absolute attempt is manifested, to place them in a favourable point of view, they are drawn with a brutal promptitude to quarrel, which is a disgrace to the well known humanity of their country.—The gentlemen of Ireland have doubtless a quick sense of honour, and, like the gentlemen of England, as well as like the gentlemen of every other high-spirited nation, are perhaps unhappily too ready to draw the sword, where they conceive themselves injured—But to make them proud of a barbarous propensity to Duelling; to make them actually delight in the effusion of blood, is to fasten a very unjust reproach upon their general character, and to render

der them univerfally obnoxious to fociety. The author of the School for Wives therefore, has given a different picture of Irifh manners, though in humble life, and flatters himfelf that thofe who are really acquainted with the original, will acknowlege it to be at leaft a tolerable refemblance.

It would be ungrateful in the higheft degree to clofe this preface, without acknowledging the very great obligations which the author has to Mr. Garrick. Every attention, which either as a manager, or as a man, he could give to the intereft of the following play, he has beftowed with the moft generous alacrity; but univerfally admired as he is at prefent, his intrinfic value will not be known, till his lofs is deplored; and the public have great reafon to wifh, that this may be a very diftant event in the annals of the theatre. The Epilogue fufficiently marks the mafterly hand from which it originated; fo does the comic commencement of the Prologue, and the elegant writer of the graver part, is a character of diftinguifhed eminence in the literary republic.

It has been remarked with great juftice, that few new pieces were ever better performed than *The School for Wives*. Mr. King, that highly-deferving favorite favourite of the town, was every thing the author could possibly wish in General Savage. Mr. Reddish acquired a very considerable share of merited reputation in Belville. Mr. Moody is unequalled in his Irishmen. Mr. Palmer, from his manner of supporting Leeson, was entitled to a much better part: And Mr. Weston in Torington was admirable. Miss Younge, in Mrs. Belville, extorted applause from the coldest auditor. Her tenderness—her force-----her pathos, were the true effusions of genius, and proved that she has no superior where the feelings are to be interested. With respect to Mrs. Abington, enough can never be said. The elegance, the vivacity, the critical nicety with which she went through Miss Walsingham, is only to be guessed at, by those who are familiar with the performance of that exquisite actress. Her Epilogue was delivered with an animation not to be conceived, and manifested the strict propriety, with which she is called the first priestess of the Comic Muse in this country.

Jan. 1, 1774.

THE SCHOOL FOR WIVES,

BEING A COMEDY IN WHICH THE LADIES ARE PARTICULARLY INTERESTED,

IT SHOULD BE ADDRESS'D TO THE FIRST ORNAMENT OF THE SEX;

AND IS THEREFORE INSCRIBED WITH THE HIGHEST ADMIRATION AND THE MOST PROFOUND REVERENCE,

TO HER MAJESTY;

NOT BECAUSE SHE IS THE GREATEST OF QUEENS,

BUT BECAUSE IN THE MILDER, AND MORE ENDEARING RELATIONS OF LIFE,

SHE IS THE BRIGHTEST PATTERN OF ALL THE FEMALE VIRTUES.

January 1, 1774.

PROLOGUE.

Spoken by Mr. KING.

NO coward he, who in this critick age,
Dares set his foot upon the dang'rous stage;
These boards, like Ice, your footing will betray,
Who can tread sure upon a slipp'ry way?
Yet some thro' five acts, slide with wond'rous skill,
Skim swift along, turn, stop, or wind at will!
Some tumble, and get up; some rise no more;
While cruel criticks watch them on the shore,
And at each stumble make a hellish roar!
A wise Philosopher, hath truly noted,
(His name I have forgot, tho' often quoted,)
That fine-spun spirits from the slightest cause,
Draw to themselves affliction, or applause:
So fares it with our Bard.---Last week he meets
Some hawkers, roaring up and down the streets,
Lives, characters, behaviour, parentage,
Of some who lately left the mortal stage!
His ears so caught the sound, and work'd his mind,
He thought his own name floated in the wind;
As thus---" Here is a faithful, true relation,
" Of the birth, parentage, and eaucation,
" Last dying speech, confession, character,
" Of the unhappy malefacterer,
" And comick poet, Thomas Addle Brain!
" Who suffer'd Monday last at Drury Lane;
" All for the price of half-penny a piece;"
Still in his ears these horrid sounds encrease!
Try'd and condemn'd, half executed too;
There stands the culprit; 'till repriev'd by you.

[going.

Enter

PROLOGUE.

Enter Miss YOUNGE.

Miss YOUNGE.

Pray give me leave—I've something now to say.

Mr. KING.

Is't at the School for Wives, *you're taught this way?*
The School for Husbands *teaches to obey.*

[*Exit.*

Miss YOUNGE.

It is a shame, good Sirs, that brother King,
To joke and laughter, should turn every thing.
Our frighted poet would have no denial,
But, begs me to say something on his trial:
The School for Wives, *as it to us belongs,*
Should for our use be guarded with our tongues.
Ladies, prepare, arm well your brows and eyes,
From those your thunder, those your light'ning flies.
Should storms be rising in the Pit---look down,
And still the waves thus, fair ones, with a frown:
Or should the Galleries for war declare;
Look up---your eyes will carry twice as far.

* *Our Bard, to noble triumphs points your way,*
Bids you in moral principles be gay;
Something he'd alter in your education,
Something which hurting you, would hurt a nation:
Ingenuous natures wish you to reclaim?
By smiling virtue you'll insure your aim:
That gilds with bliss the matrimonial hours,
And blends her laurels with the sweetest flowers.

Ye married fair! deign to attend our school,
And without usurpation *learn to rule:*
Soon will he cease mean objects to pursue,
In conscience wretched till he lives to you;
Your charms will reformation's pain beguile,
And vice receive a stab from every smile.

---

* The conclusion of the Prologue from this line is by another hand.

EPILOGUE.

Spoken by Mrs. ABINGTON.

CAN it be thought, ye wives! this scribbling fool,
Will draw you here, by calling you to School?
Does not he know, poor soul! to be directed,
Is what you hate, and more to be corrected!
Long have these walls to public fame been known,
An ancient College *to instruct the town!*
We've Schools *for* Rakes, *for* Fathers, Lovers, Wives,
For naughty girls and boys, to mend their lives:
Where some to yawn, some round about to look,
Some to be seen, few come to mind their book:
Some with high wit and humour hither run,
To sweat the masters---and they call it fun.
Some modish sparks, true stoicks, and high bred,
Come, but ne'er know what's done, or sung, or said;
Should the whole herd of criticks round them roar,
And with one voice cry out, encore! encore!
Or louder yet, off, off; no more! no more!
Should Pit, Box, Gall'ry with convulsions shake,
Still are they half asleep, nor t'other half awake:
O, ladies fair! are these fit men to wed?
Such husbands, half, had better be quite dead.
But, to return,---vain men, throughout the nation,
Boast, they alone, have College *education:*
Are not we qualify'd to take degrees?
We've caps, and gowns, nay bands too, if you please,
Cornelly's, and Almack's, our Universities!
Young female students rise, if girls of parts,
From under graduates,---mistresses of arts!
The bashful spinsters, turn important spouses,
Strive to be masters, and the heads of houses!
Will any of you here, blest with a wife,
Dispute the fact,---you dare not for your life.

Pray

EPILOGUE.

Pray tell me truly, criticks, and be free,
Do you this night prefer the Wife *to* me?
Shall Mrs. Belville *give the Play a name?*
What are her merits? a cold, smiling dame,
While I, a salamander, liv'd in flame!
Press'd by three lovers!---'twas indeed provoking!
Ladies, upon my word, it was no joking.
Can you from mortal woman more require,
Than save her fingers, and yet play with fire?
The risks I run, the partial bard upbraids;
Wives won't be taught,---be it the School for Maids.

Dramatis Personæ.

MEN.

General SAVAGE,   Mr. KING,
BELVILLE,   Mr. REDDISH,
TORRINGTON,   Mr. WESTON,
LEESON,   Mr. PALMER,
Captain SAVAGE,   Mr. BRERETON,
CONNOLLY,   Mr. MOODY,
SPRUCE,   Mr. BADDELEY,
GHASTLY,   Mr. W. PALMER.

WOMEN.

Miss WALSINGHAM,   Mrs. ABINGTON,
Mrs. BELVILLE,   Miss YOUNGE,
Lady RACHEL MILDEW,   Mrs. HOPKINS,
Mrs. TEMPEST,   Mrs. GREVILLE,
Miss LEESON,   Miss JARRATT,
MAID,   Mrs. MILLIDGE.

THE

Dramatis Personæ.

MEN.

Creon, prince,	Mr. A—.
Bertie,	Mr. Gunton.
Touchstone,	Mr. Wilkins.
Lazar,	Mr. Lacey.
Cyril,	Mr. Barrington.
Gawain,	Mr. Moore.
Basco,	Mr. Fairplay.
Chorus,	Mr. W. Lucas.

WOMEN.

Mrs. Jerningham,	Miss Jerningham.
Miss Lacey,	Miss Lacey.
Lady Constance Wrottersley,	Miss Hart.
Mrs. T—xit,	Mrs. Costar.
Miss Loron,	Miss J—son.
Fairy,	Miss Sherman.

THE

School for Wives.

ACT I.

SCENE, *an Apartment at* BELVILLE'*s*.

Enter Captain SAVAGE, *and Mifs* WALSINGHAM.

CAPT. HA! ha! ha! Well, Miſs Walſingham, this fury is going; what a noble peal ſhe has rung in Belville's ears!

Miſs WAL. Did ſhe ſee you, Captain Savage?

CAPT. No, I took care of that; for tho' ſhe is'n't married to my father, ſhe has ten times the influence of a wife, and might injure me not a little with him, if I didn't ſupport her ſide of the queſtion.

Miſs WAL. It was a pleaſant conceit of Mr. Belville, to inſinuate the poor woman was diſordered in her ſenſes!—

CAPT. And did you obſerve how the termagant's violence of temper, ſupported the probability of the charge?

Miſs WAL. Yes, ſhe became almoſt frantic in reality, when ſhe found herſelf treated like a madwoman.

CAPT.

Capt. Belville's affected surprise too, was admirable!

Miss Wal. Yes, the hypocritical composure of his countenance, and his counterfeit pity for the poor woman, were intolerable!

Capt. While that amiable creature, his wife, implicitly believed every syllable he said—

Miss Wal. And felt nothing but pity for the accuser, instead of paying the least regard to the accusation. But pray, is it really under a pretence of getting the girl upon the stage, that Belville has taken away Mrs. Tempest's neice from the people she boarded with?

Capt. It is: Belville, ever on the look out for fresh objects, met her in those primitive regions of purity, the Green-Boxes; where, discovering that she was passionately desirous of becoming an actress, he improved his acquaintance with her, in the fictitious character of an Irish manager, and she eloped last night, to be, as she imagines, the heroine of a Dublin theatre.

Miss Wal. So, then, as he has kept his real name artfully conceal'd, Mrs. Tempest can at most but suspect him of Miss Leeson's seduction.

Capt. Of no more; and this, only, from the description of the people who saw him in company with her at the play; but, I wish the affair may not have a serious conclusion; for she has a brother, a very spirited young fellow, who is a council in the Temple, and who will certainly call Belville to an account, the moment he hears of it.

Miss Wal. And what will become of the poor creature after he has deserted her?

Capt. You know that Belville is generous to profusion, and has a thousand good qualities to counterbalance this single fault of gallantry, which contaminates his character.

Miss

Miss Wal. You men! you men!—You are such wretches that there's no having a moment's satisfaction with you! and what's still more provoking, there's no having a moment's satisfaction without you!

Capt. Nay, don't think us all alike.

Miss Wal. I'll endeavour to deceive myself; for it is but a poor argument of your sincerity, to be the confidant of another's falsehood.

Capt. Nay, no more of this, my love; no people live happier than Belville and his wife; nor is there a man in England, notwithstanding all his levity, who considers his wife with a warmer degree of affection: if you have a friendship therefore, for her, let her continue in an error, so necessary to her repose, and give no hint, whatever, of his gallantries to any body.

Miss Wal. If I had no pleasure in obliging you, I have too much regard for Mrs. Belville, not to follow your advice; but you need not enjoin me so strongly on the subject, when you know I can keep a secret.

Capt. You are all goodness; and the prudence with which you have conceal'd our private engagements, has eternally oblig'd me; had you trusted the secret even to Mrs. Belville, it wou'dn't have been safe; she wou'd have told her husband, and he is such a rattleskul, that, notwithstanding all his regard for me, he wou'd have mention'd it in some moment of levity, and sent it in a course of circulation to my father.

Miss Wal. The peculiarity of your father's temper, join'd to my want of fortune, made it necessary for me to keep our engagements inviolably secret; there is no merit, therefore, either in my prudence, or in my labouring assiduously to cultivate the good opinion of the General; since both were so necesary to my own happiness; don't despise me for this acknowledgement now.

Capt. Bewitching softness!—But your goodness, I flatter myself, will be speedily rewarded; you are now such a favourite with him, that he is eternally talking of you; and I really fancy he means to propose you to me himself: for, last night, in a few minutes after he had declared you would make the best wife in the world, he seriously ask'd me if I had any aversion to matrimony?

Miss Wal. Why, that was a very great concession indeed, as he seldom stoops to consult any body's inclinations.

Capt. So it was, I assure you; for, in the army, being used to nothing but command and obedience, he removes the discipline of the parade into his family, and no more expects his orders shou'd be disputed, in matters of a domestic nature, than if they were deliver'd at the head of his regiment.

Miss Wal. And yet, Mrs. Tempest, who you say is as much a storm in her nature as her name, is disputing them eternally.

Enter Mr. and Mrs. Belville.

Bel. Well, Miss Walsingham, hav'n't we had a pretty morning's visitor?

Miss Wal. Really, I think so; and I have been asking Capt. Savage, how long the lady has been disordered in her senses?

Bel. Why will they let the poor woman abroad, without some body to take care of her?

Capt. O, she has her lucid intervals.

Miss Wal. I declare I shall be as angry with you as I am with Belville.   *(aside to the Captain.)*

Mrs. Bel. You can't think how sensibly she spoke at first.

Bel. I should have had no conception of her madness

ness, if she hadn't brought so preposterous a charge against me.

Enter a Servant.

SER. Lady Rachel Mildew, Madam, sends her compliments, and if you are not particularly engaged, will do herself the pleasure of waiting upon you.

Mrs. BEL. Our compliments, and we shall be glad to see her Ladyship. [*Ex. Servant.*

BEL. I wonder if Lady Rachel knows that Torrington came to town last night from Bath!

Mrs. BEL. I hope he has found benefit by the waters, for he is one of the best creatures existing; he's a downright parson Adams, in good nature and simplicity.

Miss WAL. Lady Rachel will be quite happy at his return, and it would be a laughable affair, if a match could be brought about between the old maid and the old bachelor.

CAPT. Mr. Torrington is too much taken up at Westminster-Hall, to think of paying his devoirs to the ladies; and too plain a speaker, I fancy, to be agreeable to Lady Rachel.

BEL. You mistake the matter widely; she is deeply smitten with him; but honest Torrington is utterly unconscious of his conquest, and modestly thinks that he has not a single attraction for any woman in the universe.

Mrs. BEL. Yet my poor aunt speaks sufficiently plain, in all conscience, to give him a different opinion of himself.

Miss WAL. Yes, and puts her charms into such repair, whenever she expects to meet him, that her cheeks look for all the world like a rasberry ice upon a ground of custard.

CAPT. I thought *Apollo* was the only god of Lady Rachel's

Rachel's idolatary, and that in her passion for poetry she had taken leave of all the less elevated affections.

BEL. O, you mistake again; the poets are eternally in love, and can by no means be calculated to describe the imaginary passions, without being very susceptible of the real ones.

Enter Servant.

SER. The man, Madam, from Tavistock-street, has brought home the dresses for the masquerade, and desires to know if there are any commands for him.

Mrs. BEL. O, bid him stay till we see the dresses.
[*Ex. Servant.*

Miss WAL. They are only Dominos.

BEL. I am glad of that; for characters are as difficult to be supported at the masquerade, as they are in real life. The last time I was at the Pantheon, a vestal virgin invited me to sup with her, and swore that her pocket had been pick'd by a Justice of peace.

Miss WAL. Nay, that was not so bad, as the Hamlet's Ghost that box'd with Henry the Eighth, and afterwards danc'd a hornpipe to the tune of Nancy Dawson. Ha! ha! ha!—We follow you, Mrs. Belville. [*Exeunt.*

Scene changes to LEESON's *Chambers in the Temple.*

Enter LEESON.

LEES. Where is this clerk of mine? Connolly!

CON. (*behind*) Here, Sir!

LEES. Have you copied the marriage settlement, as I corrected it?

CON. (*Enters with pistols*). Ay, honey, an hour ago.

LEES. What, you have been trying those pistols?

CON.

Con. By my soul, I have been firing them this half hour, without once being able to make them go off.

Lees. They are plaguy dirty.

Con. In troth, so they are: I strove to brighten them up a little, but some misfortune attends every thing I do, for the more I clane them, the dirtier they are, honey.

Lees. You have had some of our usual daily visitors for money, I suppose?

Con. You may say that; and three or four of them are now hanging about the door, that I wish handsomely hang'd any where else, for bodering us.

Lees. No joking, Connolly! my present situation is a very disagreeable one.

Con. Faith, and so it is; but who makes it disareeable? your Aunt Tempest would let you have as much money as you please, but you won't condescend to be acquainted with her, though people in this country can be very intimate friends, without seeing one anothers faces for seven years.

Lees. Do you think me base enough to receive a favour from a woman; who has disgraced her family, and stoops to be a kept mistress? you see, my sister is already ruin'd by a connection with her.

Con. Ah, Sir, a good guinea isn't the worse for coming through a bad hand; if it was, what would become of us lawyers? and by my soul, many a high head in London would, at this minute, be very low, if they hadn't recieved favours even from much worse people than kept mistresses.

Lees. Others, Connolly, may prostitute their honour, as they please; mine is my chief possession, and I must take particular care of it.

Con. Honour, to be sure, is a very fine thing, Sir; but I don't see how it is to be taken care of, without a little money; your honour, to my knowledge, has'n't been in your own possession these two years,

years, and the devil a crum can you honeftly fwear by, till you get it out of the hands of your creditors.

LEES. I have given you a licence to talk, Connolly, because I know you faithful; but I hav'n't given you a liberty to fport with my misfortunes.

CON. You know I'd die to ferve you, Sir; but of what ufe is your giving me leave to fpake, if you oblige me to hould my tongue? 'tis out of pure love and affection that I put you in mind of your misfortunes.

LEES. Well, Connolly, a few days will, in all probability, enable me to redeem my honour, and to reward your fidelity; the lovely Emily, you know, has half confented to embrace the firft opportunity of flying with me to Scotland, and the paltry trifles I owe, will not be mifs'd in her Fortune.

CON. But, dear Sir, confider you are going to fight a duel this very evening, and if you fhou'd be kilt, I fancy you will find it a little difficult, to run away afterwards with the lovely Emily.

LEES. If I fall, there will be an end to my misfortunes.

CON. But furely it will not be quite genteel, to go out of the world without paying your debts.

LEES. But how fhall I ftay in the world, Connolly, without punifhing Belville for ruining my fifter?

CON. O, the devil fly away with this honour; an ounce of common fenfe, is worth a whole fhip load of it, if we muft prefer a bullet or a halter, to a fine young lady and a great fortune.

LEES. We'll talk no more on the fubject at prefent. Take this letter to Mr. Belville; deliver it into his own hand, be fure; and bring me an anfwer: make hafte; for I fhall not ftir out till you come back.

CON. By my foul, I wifh you may be able to ftir out then, honey.—O, but that's true!

LEES. What's the matter?

CON. Why, Sir, the gentleman I laft liv'd clerk with,

with, died lately and left me a legacy of twenty guineas—

LEES. What! is Mr. Stanley dead?

CON. Faith, his friends have behav'd very unkindly if he is not, for they have buried him these six weeks.

LEES. And what then?

CON. Why, Sir, I received my little legacy this morning, and if you'd be so good as to keep it for me, I'd be much oblig'd to you.

LEES. Connolly, I understand you, but I am already shamefully in your debt: you've had no money from me this age.—

CON. O Sir, that does not signify; if you are not kilt in this damn'd duel, you'll be able enough to pay me: if you are, I shan't want it.

LEES. Why so, my poor fellow?

CON. Because, tho' I am but your clerk, and tho' I think fighting the most foolish thing upon earth, I'm as much a gintleman as yourself, and have as much right to commit a murder in the way of duelling.

LEES. And what then? You have no quarrel with Mr. Belville?

CON. I shall have a damn'd quarrel with him tho' if you are kilt: your death shall be reveng'd, depend upon it, so let that content you.

LEES. My dear Connolly, I hope I shan't want such a proof of your affection.—How he distresses me!

CON. You will want a second, I suppose, in this affair: I stood second to my own brother, in the Fifteen Acres, and tho' that has made me detest the very thought of duelling ever since; yet if you want a friend, I'll attend you to the field of death with a great deal of satisfaction.

LEES. I thank you, Connolly, but I think it extremely wrong in any man who has a quarrel, to ex-

C pose

pose his friend to difficulties; we shou'dn't seek for redress, if we are not equal to the task of fighting our own battles; and I choose you particularly, to carry my letter because, you may be supposed ignorant of the contents, and thought to be acting only in the ordinary course of your business.

Con. Say no more about it, honey; I will be back with you presently. (*going, returns.*) I put the twenty guineas in your pocket, before you were up, Sir; and I don't believe you'd look for such a thing there, if I wasn't to tell you of it. [*Exit.*

Lees. This faithful, noble-hearted creature!— but let me fly from thought; the business I have to execute, will not bear the test of reflection. [*Exit.*

Re-enter Connolly.

Con. As this is a challenge, I shou'dn't go without a sword; come down, little tickle-pitcher. (*Takes a sword.*) Some people may think me very conceited now; but as the dirtiest black legs in town can wear one without being stared at, I don't think it can suffer any disgrace by the side of an honest man.
[*Exit.*

SCENE *changes to an Apartment at* Belville's.

Enter Mrs. Belville.

Mrs. Bel. How strangely this affair of Mrs. Tempest hangs upon my spirits, tho' I have every reason, from the tenderness, the politeness, and the generosity of Mr. Belville, as well as from the woman's behaviour, to believe the whole charge the result of a disturb'd imagination.—Yet suppose it should be actually true:—heigho!—well, suppose it shou'd;—I wou'd endeavour—I think I wou'd endeavour to keep my temper:—a frowning face never recovered a heart that was not to be fix'd with a smiling one:—but women, in general, forget this grand article of the matrimonial

trimonial creed entirely; the dignity of infulted virtue obliges them to play the fool, whenever their Corydons play the libertine;—and poh! they muft pull down the houfe about the traitor's ears, tho' they are themfelves to be crufh'd in pieces by the ruins.

Enter a Servant.

SER. Lady Rachel Mildew, madam. [*Exit Ser.*

Enter Lady RACHEL MILDEW.

Lady RACH. My dear, how have you done fince the little eternity of my laft feeing you. Mr. Torrington is come to town, I hear.

Mrs. BEL. He is, and muft be greatly flattered to find that your Ladyfhip has made him the hero of your new comedy.

Lady RACH. Yes, I have drawn him as he is, an honeft practitioner of the law; which is I fancy no very common character.—

Mrs. BEL. And it muft be a vaft acquifition to the Theatre.

Lady RACH. Yet the managers of both houfes have refufed my play; have refufed it peremptorily! tho' I offer'd to make them a prefent of it.

Mrs. BEL. That's very furprizing, when you offer'd to make them a prefent of it.

Lady RACH. They alledge that the audiences are tired of crying at comedies; and infift that my Defpairing Shepherdefs is abfolutely too difmal for reprefentation.

Mrs. BEL. What, tho' you have introduced a lawyer in a new light?

Lady RACH. Yes, and have a boarding-fchool romp, that flaps her mother's face, and throws a bafon of fcalding water at her governefs.

Mrs. BEL. Why, furely, thefe are capital jokes!

Lady Rach. But the managers can't find them out.—However, I am determined to bring it out somewhere; and I have discover'd such a treasure for my boarding-school romp, as exceeds the most sanguine expectation of criticism.

Mrs. Bel. How fortunate!

Lady Rach. Going to Mrs. Le Blond, my millener's, this morning, to see some contraband silks, (for you know there's a foreign minister just arriv'd) I heard a loud voice rehearsing Juliet, from the dining-room; and upon enquiry found that it was a country girl, just elop'd from her friends in town, to go upon the stage with an Irish manager.

Mrs. Bel. Ten to one, the strange woman's neice, who has been here this morning. *(aside.*

Lady Rach. Mrs. Le Blond has some doubts about the manager it seems, though she hasn't seen him yet, because the apartments are very expensive, and were taken by a fine gentleman out of livery.

Mrs. Bel. What am I to think of this?—Pray, Lady Rachel, as you have convers'd with this young actress, I suppose you could procure me a sight of her.

Lady Rach. This moment if you will, I am very intimate with her already; but pray keep the matter a secret from your husband, for he is so witty, you know, upon my passion for the drama, that I shall be teized to death by him.

Mrs. Bel. O, you may be very sure that your secret is safe, for I have a most particular reason to keep it from Mr. Belville; but he is coming this way with Captain Savage, let us at present avoid him. [*Exeunt.*

Enter Belville, *and Captain* Savage.

Capt. You are a very strange man, Belville; you are for ever tremblingly solicitous about the happiness

piness of your wife, yet for ever endangering it by your passion for variety.

BEL. Why, there is certainly a contradiction between my principles and my practice; but, if ever you marry, you'll be able to reconcile it perfectly. Possession, Savage! O, possession, is a miserable whetter of the appetite in love! and I own myself so sad a fellow, that though I wou'dn't exchange Mrs. Belville's mind for any woman's upon earth, there is scarcely a woman's person upon earth, which is not to me a stronger object of attraction.

CAPT. Then perhaps in a little time you'll be weary of Miss Leeson?

BEL. To be sure I shall; though to own the truth, I have not yet carried my point conclusively with the little monkey.

CAPT. Why how the plague has she escap'd a moment in your hands?

BEL. By a mere accident.—She came to the lodgings, which my man Spruce prepar'd for her, rather unexpectedly last night, so that I happened to be engaged particularly in another quarter—you understand me—and the damn'd aunt found me so much employment all the morning, that I could only send a message by Spruce, promising to call upon her the first moment I had to spare in the course of the day.

CAPT. And so your are previously satisfied that you shall be tired of her.

BEL. Tir'd of her?—Why I am at this moment in pursuit of fresh game, against the hour of satiety:—Game that you know to be exquisite! and I fancy I shall bring it down, though it is closely guarded by a deal of that pride, which passes for virtue with the generallity of your mighty good people.

CAPT. Indeed! and may a body know this wonder?

BEL.

BEL. You are to be trusted with any thing, for you are the closest fellow I ever knew, and the rack itself would hardly make you discover one of your own secrets to any body—what do you think of Miss Walsingham?

CAPT. Miss Walsingham?—Death and the devil!
(aside.)

BEL. Miss. Walsingham:

CAPT. Why surely she has not received your addresses with any degree of approbation?

BEL. With every degree of approbation I cou'd expect.

CAPT. She has?

BEL. Ay: Why this news surprises you?

CAPT. It does indeed!

BEL. Ha, ha, ha! I can't help laughing to think what a happy dog Miss Walsingham's husband is likely to be!

CAPT. A very happy dog, truly!

BEL. She's a delicious girl, is'n't she, Savage?— but she'll require a little more trouble;—for a fine woman, like a fortified town, to speak in your father's language, demands a regular siege; and we must even allow her the honours of war, to magnify the greatness of our own victory.

CAPT. Well, it amazes me how you gay fellows ever have the presumption to attack a woman of principle; Miss Walsingham has no apparent levity of any kind about her.

BEL. No; but she continued in my house, after I had whispered my passion in her ear, and gave me a second opportunity of addressing her improperly; what greater encouragement cou'd I desire?

Enter SPRUCE.

Well, Spruce, what are your commands?

SPRUCE. My Lady is just gone out with Lady Rachel, Sir.   BEL.

BEL. I underſtand you.

SPRUCE. I believe you do. (*Aſide*.) [*Exit*.

CAPT. What is the Engliſh of theſe ſignificant looks between Spruce and you?

BEL. Only that Miſs Walſingham is left alone, and that I have now an opportunity of entertaining her; you muſt excuſe me, Savage; you muſt upon my ſoul; but not a word of this affair to any body; becauſe when I ſhake her off my hands, there may be fools enough to think of her, upon terms of honourable matrimony. [*Exit*

CAPT. So, here's a diſcovery! a precious diſcovery! and while I have been racking my imagination, and ſacrificing my intereſt, to promote the happineſs of this woman, ſhe has been liſtening to the addreſſes of another; to the addreſſes of a married man! the huſband of her friend, and the immediate friend of her intended huſband!—By Belville's own account, however, ſhe has not yet proceeded to any criminal lengths---But why did ſhe keep the affair a ſecret from me? or why did ſhe continue in his houſe after a repeated declaration of his unwarrantable attachment?---What's to be done?---If I open my engagement with her to Belville, I am ſure he will inſtantly deſiſt;—but then her honour is left in a ſtate extremely queſtionable—It ſhall be ſtill concealed—While it remains unknown, Belville will himſelf tell me every thing;—and doubt, upon an occaſion of this nature, is infinitely more inſupportable than the downright falſehood of the woman whom we love.

 [*Exit*.

The END *of the* FIRST ACT.

ACT II.

SCENE, *an Apartment in General* SAVAGE'*s House.*

Enter General SAVAGE, *and* TORRINGTON.

GEN. ZOUNDS! Torrington, give me quarter, when I surrender up my sword: I own that for these twenty years, I have been suffering all the inconveniences of marriage, without tasting any one of its comforts, and rejoicing in an imaginary freedom, while I was really grovelling in chains.

TOR. In the dirtiest chains upon earth;—yet you wou'dn't be convinc'd, but laugh'd at all your married acquaintance as slaves, when not one of them put up with half so much from the worst wife, as you were oblig'd to crouch under, from a kept mistress.

GEN. 'Tis too true. But, you know, she sacrificed much for me;—you know that she was the widow of a colonel, and refus'd two very advantageous matches on my account.—

TOR. If she was the widow of a judge, and had refused a high chancellor, she was still a devil incarnate, and you were of course a madman to live with her.

GEN. You don't remember her care of me when I have been sick.—

TOR. I recollect, however, her usage of you in health, and you may easily find a tenderer nurse, when you are bound over by the gout or the rheumatism.

GEN.

Gen. Well, well, I agree with you that she is a devil incarnate; but I am this day determin'd to part with her for ever.

Tor. Not you indeed.

Gen. What, don't I know my own mind?

Tor. Not you indeed, when she is in the question; with every body else, your resolution is as unalterable as a determination in the house of peers; but Mrs. Tempest is your fate, and she reverses your decrees with as little difficulty as a fraudulent debtor now-a-days procures his certificate under a commission of bankruptcy.

Gen. Well if, like the Roman Fabius, I conquer by delay, in the end, there will be no great reason to find fault with my generalship. The proposal of parting now comes from herself.

Tor. O, you darn't make it for the life of you.

Gen. You must know that this morning we had a smart cannonanading on Belville's account, and she threatens, as I told you before, to quit my house if I don't challenge him for taking away her neice.

Tor. That fellow is the very devil among the women, and yet there isn't a man in England fonder of his wife.

Gen. Poh, if the young minx hadn't surrender'd to him, she would have capitulated to somebody else, and I shall at this time be doubly obliged to him, if he is any ways instrumental in getting the aunt off my hands.

Tor. Why at this time?

Gen. Because to shew you how fix'd my resolution is to be a keeper no longer, I mean to marry immediately.

Tor. And can't you avoid being press'd to death, like a felon who refuses to plead, without incurring a sentence of perpetual imprisonment?

Gen. I fancy you would yourself have no objection to a perpetual imprisonment in the arms of Miss Walsingham.

Tor. But have you any reason to think that upon examination in a case of love, she would give a favourable reply to your interrogatories?

Gen. The greatest—do you think I'd hazard such an engagement without being perfectly sure of my ground? Notwithstanding my present connection won't suffer me to see a modest woman at my own house—She always treats me with particular attention whenever I visit at Belville's, or meet her any where else—If fifty young fellows are present, she directs all her assiduities to the old soldier, and my son has a thousand times told me that she professes the highest opinion of my understanding.

Tor. And truly you give a notable proof of your understanding, in thinking of a woman almost young enough to be your grand-daughter.

Gen. Nothing like an experienc'd chief to command in any garrison.

Tor. Recollect the state of your present citadel.

Gen. Well, if I am blown up by my own mine, I shall be the only sufferer—There's another thing I want to talk of, I am going to marry my son to Miss Moreland.

Tor. Miss Moreland!—

Gen. Belville's sister.—

Tor. O, ay, I remember that Moreland had got a good estate to assume the name of Belville.

Gen. I have'nt yet mention'd the matter to my son, but I settled the affair with the girl's mother yesterday, and she only waits to communicate it to Belville, who is her oracle, you know.

Tor. And are you sure the captain will like her?

Gen. I am not so unreasonable as to insist upon his liking her, I shall only insist upon his marrying her.

Tor. What, whether he likes her or not?

Gen.

Gen. When I issue my orders, I expect them to be obey'd; and don't look for an examination into their propriety.

Tor. What a delightful thing it must be to live under a military government, where a man is not to be troubled with the exercise of his understanding.

Gen. Miss Moreland has thirty thousand pounds—That's a large sum of ammunition money.

Tor. Ay, but a marriage merely on the score of fortune, is only gilding the death-warrant sent down for the execution of a prisoner. However as I know your obstinate attachment to what you once resolve, I shan't pretend to argue with you; where are the papers which you want me to consider?

Gen. They are in my library—File off with me to the next room and they shall be laid before you—But first I'll order the chariot, for the moment I have your opinion; I purpose to sit down regularly before Miss Walsingham—who waits there?

Enter a servant.

Gen. Is Mrs. Tempest at home?

Serv. Yes, Sir, just come in, and just going out again.

Gen. Very well; order the chariot to be got ready.

Serv. Sir, one of the pannels was broke last night at the Opera-house.

Gen. Sir, I d'dn't call to have the pleasure of your conversation, but to have obedience paid to my orders.

Tor. Go order the chariot, you blockhead.

Serv. With the broken pannel, Sir.

Gen. Yes, you rascal, if both pannels were broke, and the back shattered to pieces.

Serv. The coachman thinks that one of the wheels is damag'd, Sir.

Gen. Don't attempt to reason, you dog, but execute your orders.——Bring the chariot without the wheels—if you can't bring it with them.

Tor. Ay bring it, if you reduce it to a sledge, and let your master look like a malefactor for high treason, on his journey to Tyburn.

Enter Mrs. Tempest.

Mrs. Temp. General Savage, is the house to be for ever a scene of noise with your domineering?—The chariot shan't be brought—it won't be fit for use 'till it is repaired—and John, shall drive it this very minute to the coach-makers.

Gen. Nay, my dear, if it isn't fit for use that's another thing.

Tor. Here's the experienced chief that's fit to command in any garrison.   *(aside.)*

Gen. Go order me the coach then.   *(to the Ser.*

Mrs. Temp. You can't have the coach.

Gen. And why so, my love.

Mrs. Temp. Because I want it for myself.—Robert, get a hack for your master—tho' indeed I don't see what business he has out of the house.

[*Exeunt Mrs. Tempest and Robert.*

Tor. When you issue your orders, you expect them to be obey'd, and don't look for an examination into their propriety.

Gen. The fury!—this has steel'd me against her for ever, and nothing on earth can now prevent me from drumming her out immediately.

Mrs. Temp. *(behind)* An unreasonable old fool—But I'll make him know who governs this house!

Gen. Zounds! here she comes again; she has been lying in ambuscade, I suppose, and has over heard us.

Tor. What if she has? you are steel'd against her for ever.

Gen. No, she's not coming—she's going down stairs;

stairs;—and now, dear Torrington, you must be as silent as a sentinel on an out-post about this affair. If that virago was to hear a syllable of it, she might perhaps attack Miss Walsingham in her very camp, and defeat my whole plan of operations.

Tor. I thought you were determin'd to drum her out immediately. [*Exeunt.*

The SCENE *changes to* BELVILLE'S.

Enter Miss WALSINGHAM, *followed by* BELVILLE.

Miss WAL. I beg, Sir, that you will insult me no longer with solicitations of this nature—Give me proofs of your sincerity indeed! What proofs of sincerity can your situation admit of, if I could be even weak enough to think of you with partiality at all?

BEL. If our affections, Madam, were under the government of our reason, circumstanced as I am, this unhappy bosom wouldn't be torn by passion for Miss Walsingham.—Had I been bless'd with your acquaintance, before I saw Mrs. Belville, my hand as well as my heart, wou'd have been humbly offer'd to your acceptance—fate, however, has ordered it otherwise, and it is cruel to reproach me with that situation as a crime, which ought to be pitied as my greatest misfortune.

Miss WAL. He's actually forcing tears into his eyes.—However, I'll mortify him severely. (*aside.*)

BEL. But such proofs of sincerity as my situation can admit of, you shall yourself command, as my only business in existence is to adore you.

Miss WAL. His only business in existence to adore me. (*aside.*)

BEL. Prostrate at your feet, my dearest Miss Walsingham (*kneeling*) behold a heart eternally devoted to your service.—You have too much good sense, Madam, to be the slave of custom, and too much humanity not to pity the wretchedness you have caused.

caused.—Only, therefore, say that you commiserate my sufferings—I'll ask no more—and surely that may be said, without any injury to your purity, to snatch even an enemy from distraction—where's my handkerchief? *(aside.*

Miss Wal. Now to answer in his own way, and to make him ridiculous to himself—*(aside.)* If I thought, if I could think *(affecting to weep)* that these protestations were real.

Bel. How can you, Madam, be so unjust to your own merit? how can you be so cruelly doubtful of my solemn asseverations?—Here I again kneel, and swear eternal love!

Miss Wal. I don't know what to say—but there is one proof—*(affecting to weep.)*

Bel. Name it, my angel, this moment, and make me the happiest of mankind!

Miss Wal. Swear to be mine for ever.

Bel. I have sworn it a thousand times, my charmer; and I will swear it to the last moment of my life.

Miss Wal. Why then—but don't look at me I beseech you—I don't know how to speak it---

Bel. The delicious emotion—do not check the generous tide of tenderness that fills me with such extasy.

Miss Wal. You'll despise me for this weakness.

Bel. This weakness—this generosity which will demand my everlasting gratitude.

Miss Wal. I am a fool—but there is a kind of fatality in this affair—and I do consent to go off with you.

Bel. Eternal blessings on your condescension.

Miss Wal. You are irresistible, and I am ready to fly with you to any part of the world.

Bel. Fly to any part of the world indeed—you shall fly by yourself then; *(aside.)* You are the most

most lovely, the most tender creature in the world, and thus again let me thank you: O, Miss Walsingham, I cannot express how happy you've made me!—But where's the necessity of our leaving England?——

Miss WAL. I thought he wouldn't like to go abroad—*(aside.)* That I may possess the pleasure of your company unrival'd.

BEL. I must cure her of this taste for travelling—
(aside.)

Miss WAL. You don't answer, Mr. Belville?

BEL. Why I was turning the consequence of your proposal in my thoughts, as going off—going off—you know.——

Miss WAL. Why going off, you know, is going off—And what objections can you have to going off?

BEL. Why going off, will subject you at a certainty, to the slander of the world; whereas by staying at home, we may not only have numberless opportunities of meeting, but at the same time prevent suspicion it self, from ever breathing on your reputation.

Miss WAL. I didn't dream of your starting any difficulties, Sir.—Just now I was dearer to you than all the world.

BEL. And so you are, by heav'n!

Miss WAL. Why won't you sacrifice the world then at once to obtain me?

BEL. Surely, my dearest life, you must know the necessity, which every man of honour is under, of keeping up his character?

Miss WAL. So, here's this fellow swearing to ten thousand lies, and yet talking very gravely about his honour and his character. *(aside.)* Why, to be sure in these days, Mr. Belville, the instances of conjugal infidelity are so very scarce, and men of fashion are so remarkable for a tender attachment to their wives, that I don't wonder at your circumspection---But do
you

you think I can stoop to accept you by halves, or admit of any partnership in your heart?

BEL. O you must do more than that, if you have any thing to say to me. (*aside.*) Surely, Madam, when you know my whole soul unalterably your own, you will permit me to preserve those appearances with the world, which are indispensibly requisite---Mrs. Belville is a most excellent woman, however it may be my fortune to be devoted to another---Her happiness, besides, constitutes a principal part of my felicity, and if I was publicly to forsake her, I should be hunted as a monster from society.

Miss WAL. Then, I suppose, it is by way of promoting Mrs. Belville's repose, Sir, that you make love to other women; and by way of shewing the nicety of your honour, that you attempt the purity of such as your own roof, peculiarly, intitles to protection. For the honour intended to me—thus low to the ground, I thank you, Mr. Belville.

BEL. Laugh'd at, by all the stings of mortification!

Miss WAL. Good bye.—Don't let this accident mortify your vanity too much;—but take care, the next time you vow everlasting love, that the object is neither tender enough to sob—sob—at your distress; nor provoking enough to make a proposal of leaving England.—How greatly a little common sense can lower these fellows of extraordinary impudence?
[*Exit.*

BEL. (*alone.*) So then, I am fairly taken in, and she has been only diverting herself with me all this time:—however, lady fair, I may chance to have the laugh in a little time on my side; for if you can sport in this manner about the flame, I think it must in the run lay hold of your wings:—what shall I do in this affair?—She sees the matter in its true light, and there's no good to be expected from thumping of bosoms, or squeezing white handkerchiefs;—no these
won't

won't do with women of sense, and in a short time, they'll be ridiculous to the very babies of a boarding-school.

Enter Captain SAVAGE.

CAPT. Well, Belville, what news? You have had a fresh opportunity with Miss Walsingham.

BEL. Why, faith, Savage, I've had a most extraordinary scene with her, and yet have but little reason to brag of my good fortune, tho' she offer'd, in express terms to run away with me.

CAPT. Prith'ee explain yourself, man; she cou'dn't surely be so shameless!

BEL. O, her offering to run away with me, was by no means the worst part of the affair.

CAPT. No, then it must be damn'd bad indeed! but prith'ee, hurry to an explanation.

BEL. Why then, the worst part of the affair is, that she was laughing at me the whole time; and made this proposal of an elopement, with no other view, than to shew me in strong colours to myself, as a very dirty fellow to the best wife in England.

CAPT. I am easy. *(aside.*

Enter SPRUCE.

SPRUCE. Sir, there is an Irish gentleman below with a letter for you, who will deliver it to nobody but yourself.

BEL. Shew him up then.

SPRUCE. Yes, Sir. [*Exit.*

CAPT. It may be on business Belville, I'll take my leave of you.

BEL. O, by no means; I can have no business which I desire to keep from you, tho' you are the arrant'st miser of your confidence upon earth, and wou'd rather trust your life in any body's hands, than even a paltry amour with the apprentice of a millener.

E *Ente*

Enter CONNOLLY.

CON. Gintlemin, your moſt obedient; pray which of you is Mr. Belville?

BEL. My name is Belville, at your ſervice, Sir.

CON. I have a little bit of a letter for you, Sir.

BEL. (*Reads.*)

 S I R,

The people where Miſs Leeſon lately lodg'd, aſſerting poſitively that you have taken her away in a fictitious character, the brother of that unhappy girl, thinks himſelf oblig'd to demand ſatisfaction, for the injury which you have done his family; tho' a ſtranger to your perſon, he is ſufficiently acquainted with your reputation for ſpirit, and ſhall, therefore, make no doubt of ſeeing you with a caſe of piſtols, near the Ring in Hyde Park, at eight o'clock this evening, to anſwer the claims of

To Craggs Belville, Eſq.   George Leeſon.

CAPT. Eight o'clock in the evening! 'tis a ſtrange time!

CON. Why ſo, honey? A fine evening is as good a time for a bad action as a fine morning; and if a man of ſenſe can be ſuch a fool as to fight a duel, he ſhou'd never ſleep upon the matter, for the more he thinks of it, the more he muſt feel himſelf aſham'd of his reſolution.

BEL. A pretty letter!

CON. O yes, an invitation to a brace of bullets is a very pretty thing.

BEL. For a challenge, however, 'tis very civilly written!

CON. Faith, if it was written to me, I ſhou'dn't be very fond of ſuch civility; I wonder he doesn't ſign himſelf, your moſt obedient ſervant.

            CAPT.

Capt. I told you Leeson's character, and what wou'd become of this damn'd bufinefs; but your affairs—are they fettled, Belville?

Bel. O they are always fettled—for as this is a country where people occafionally die, I take conftant care to be prepared for contingencies.

Con. Occafionally die!—I'll be very much oblig'd to you, Sir, if you tell me the country where people do not die? for I'll immediately go and end my days there.

Bel. Ha! ha! ha!

Con. Faith, you may laugh gintlemin, but tho' I am a foolifh Irifhman, and come about a foolifh piece of bufinefs, I'd prefer a fnug birth in this world, bad as it is, to the finest coffin in all Chriftendom.

Bel. I am furpris'd, Sir, that thinking in this manner, you would be the bearer of a challenge.

Con. And well you may, Sir.—But we muft often take a pleafure in ferving our friends, by doing things that are very difagreeable to us.

Capt. Then you think Mr. Leefon much to blame, perhaps, for hazarding his life where he can by no means repair the honour of his fifter.

Con. Indeed and I do—But I fhall think this gintleman, begging his pardon, much more to blame for meeting him.

Bel. And why fo, Sir—You woudn't have me difappoint your friend?

Con. Faith, and that I wou'd—He, poor lad, may have fome reafon at prefent to be tir'd of the world, but you have a fine eftate, a fine wife, a fine parcel of children.—In fhort, honey, you have every thing to make you fond of living, and the devil burn me, was I in your cafe, if I'd ftake my own happinefs agrinft the mifery of any man.

Bel. I am very much oblig'd to your advice, Sir, tho' on the prefent occafion I cannot adopt it; be fo

good

good as to prefent my compliments to your friend, and tell him I fhall certainly do myfelf the honour of attending his appointment.

Con. Why then upon my foul I am very forry for it.

Capt. 'Tis not very cuftomary, Sir, with gentlemen of Ireland to oppofe an affair of honour.

Con. They are like the gintlemin of England, Sir, they are brave to a fault; yet I hope to fee the day that it will be infamous to draw the fwords of either, against any body but the enemies of their country.
[*Exit.*

Bel. I am quite charmed with this honeft Hibernian, and would almoft fight a duel for the pleafure of his acquaintance.

Capt. Come, ftep with me a little, and let us confider, whether there may not be fome method of accommodating this curfed bufinefs.

Bel. Poh! don't be uneafy upon my account; my character, with regard to affairs of this nature, is unhappily too well eftablifhed, and you may be fure that I fhan't fight with Leefon.

Capt. No---you have injured him greatly?

Bel. The very reafon of all others why I fhould not cut his throat.   [*Exeunt.*

Enter Spruce.

Spruce. What, the devil, this mafter of mine has got a a duel upon his hands! Zounds! I am forry for that; he is a prince of a fellow! and a good fubject muft always love his prince, though he may now and then be a little out of humour with his actions.

Enter General Savage.

Gen. Your hall-door ftanding open, Spruce, and none of your fentinels being on guard, I have furprifed your camp thus far without refiftance: Where is your mafter?

Spruce.

SPRUCE. Juſt gone out with Captain Savage, Sir.

GEN. Is your lady at home?

SPRUCE. No, Sir, but Miſs Walſingham is at home; ſhall I inform her of your viſit?

GEN. There is no occaſion to inform her of it, for here ſhe is, Spruce. [*Exit Spruce.*

Enter Miſs WALSINGHAM.

Miſs WAL. General Savage, your moſt humble ſervant.

GEN. My dear Miſs Walſingham, it is rather cruel that you ſhould be left at home by yourſelf, and yet I am greatly rejoic'd to find you at preſent without company.

Miſs WAL. I can't but think myſelf in the beſt company, when I have the honour of your converſation, General.

GEN. You flatter me too much, Madam; yet I am come to talk to you on a ſerious affair, Miſs Walſingham; an affair of importance to me and to yourſelf: Have you leiſure to favour me with a ſhort audience, if I beat a parley?

Miſs WAL. Any thing of importance to you, Sir, is always ſufficient to command my leiſure.—'Tis as the Captain ſuſpected. (*aſide.*

GEN. You tremble, my lovely girl, but don't be alarmed; for though my buſineſs is of an important nature, I hope it won't be of a diſagreeable one.

Miſs WAL. And yet I am greatly agitated. (*aſide.*

GEN. Soldiers, Miſs Walſingham, are ſaid to be generally favour'd by the kind partiality of the ladies.

Miſs WAL. The ladies are not without gratitude, Sir, to thoſe who devote their lives peculiarly to the ſervice of their country.

GEN. Generouſly ſaid, Madam: Then give me leave, without any maſked battery, to aſk, if the heart

of

of an honest soldier is a prize at all worth your acceptance.

Miss WAL. Upon my word, Sir, there's no masked battery in this question.

GEN. I am as fond of a coup de main, Madam, in love, as in war, and hate the tedious method of sapping a town, when there is a possibility of entering sword in hand.

Miss WAL. Why really, Sir, a woman may as well know her own mind, when she is first summoned by the trumpet of a lover, as when she undergoes all the tiresome formality of a siege. You see I have caught your own mode of conversing, General.

GEN. And a very great compliment I consider it, Madam: But now that you have candidly confess'd an acquaintance with your own mind, answer me with that frankness for which every body admires you so much. Have you any objection to change the name of Walsingham?

Miss WAL. Why then frankly, General Savage, I say, no.

GEN. Ten thousand thanks to you for this kind declaration.

Miss WAL. I hope you won't think it a forward one.

GEN. I'd sooner see my son run away in the day of battle;—I'd sooner think Lord Russell was bribed by Lewis the XIVth, and sooner villify the memory of Algernoon Sidney.

Miss WAL. How unjust it was ever to suppose the General a tyrannical father! *aside.*

GEN. You have told me condescendingly, Miss Walsingham, that you have no objection to change your name, I have but one question more to ask.

Miss WAL. Pray propose it.

GEN. Would the name of Savage be disagreeable to you?—Speak frankly again, my dear girl!

Miss WAL. Why then again I frankly say, no.

GEN.

Gen. You make me too happy; and though I shall readily own, that a proposal of this nature would come with more propriety from my son---

Miss Wal. I am much better pleas'd that you make the proposal yourself, Sir.

Gen. You are too good to me.—Torrington thought that I should meet with a repulse. (*aside.*

Miss Wal. Have you communicated this business to the Captain, Sir?

Gen. No, my dear Madam, I did not think that at all necessary. I have always been attentive to the Captain's happiness, and I propose that he shall be married in a few days.

Miss Wal. What, whether I will or no?

Gen. O you can have no objection.

Miss Wal. I must be consulted, however, about the day, General: but nothing in my power shall be wanting to make him happy.

Gen. Obliging loveliness!

Miss Wal. You may imagine, that if I was not previously imprest in favour of your proposal, it wou'd not have met my concurrence so readily.

Gen. Then you own that I had a previous friend in the garrison.

Miss Wal. I don't blush to acknowledge it, when I consider the accomplishments of the object, Sir.

Gen. O this is too much, Madam; the principle merit of the object is his passion for Miss Walsingham.

Miss Wal. Don't say that, General, I beg of you, for I don't think there are many women in the kingdom, who could behold him with indifference.

Gen. Ah, you flattering, flattering angel!—and yet, by the memory of Marlborough, my lovely girl, it was the idea of a prepossession on your part, which encouraged me to hope for a favourable reception.

Miss WAL. Then I must have been very indiscreet, for I labour'd to conceal that prepossession as much as possible.

GEN. You cou'dn't conceal it from me! you cou'dn't conceal it from me!—The female heart is a field which I am thoroughly acquainted with, and which has more than once been a witness to my victories, Madam.

Miss WAL. I don't at all doubt your success with the ladies, General; but as we now understand one another so perfectly, you will give me leave to retire.

GEN. One word, my dear creature, and no more; I shall wait upon you sometime to day, with Mr. Torrington, about the necessary settlements.

Miss WAL. You must do as you please, General, you are invincible in every thing.

GEN. And if you please, we'll keep every thing a profound secret, 'till the articles are all settled, and the definitive treaty ready for execution.

Miss WAL You may be sure, that delicacy will not suffer me to be communicate on the subject, Sir.

GEN. Then you leave every thing to my management.

Miss WAL. I can't trust a more noble negociator.
[*Exit.*

GEN. The day's my own. (*sings.*) Britons, strike home! strike home! Revenge, &c.   [*Exit singing.*

END *of the* SECOND ACT.

ACT III.

SCENE, *Miss* LEESON's *Lodgings.*

Enter Lady RACHEL MILDEW, *Mrs.* BELVILLE, *and Miss* LEESON.

Lady RACH. WELL, Mrs. Belville, I am extremely glad you agree with me, in opinion of this young lady's qualifications for the stage. Don't you think she'd play Miss Headstrong admirably in my comedy?

Mrs. BEL. Yes, indeed, I think she possesses a natural fund of spirit, very much adapted to the character.—'Tis impossible, surely, that this hoyden can have a moment's attraction for Mr. Belville?
(aside.

Miss LEES. You are very obliging, ladies; but I have no turn for comedy; my fort is tragedy entirely.

Alphonso!—O, Alphonso! to thee I call. &c.

Lady RACH. But, my dear, is there none of our comedies to your taste?

Miss LEES. O, yes; some of the sentimental ones are very pretty, there's such little difference between them and tragedies.

Lady RACH. And pray, my dear, how long have you been engaged to Mr. Frankly?

Miss LEES. I only came away last night, and hav'n't seen Mr. Frankly since, tho' I expect him every moment.

F   *Mrs.*

Mrs. BEL. Laſt night! juſt as Mrs. Tempeſt mentioned. (*aſide.*

Lady RACH. You had the concurrence of your friends?

Miſs LEES. Not I, Madam. – Mr. Frankly ſaid, I had too much genius to mind my friends, and as I ſhould want nothing from them, there was no occaſion to conſult them in the affair.

Lady RACH. Then Oſbaldiſton is not your real name, perhaps?

Miſs LEES. O no, nor do I tell my real name: I choſe Oſbaldiſton, becauſe it was a long one, and wou'd make a ſtriking appearance in the bills.

Mrs. BEL. I wiſh we cou'd ſee Mr. Frankly.

Miſs LEES. Perhaps you may, Madam, for he deſigns to give me a leſſon every day, 'till we are ready to ſet off for Ireland.

Lady RACH. Suppoſe then, my dear, you wou'd oblige us with a ſcene in Juliet, by way of ſhewing your proficiency to Mrs. Belville.

Miſs LEES. Will you ſtand up for Romeo?

Lady RACH. With all my heart, and I'll give you ſome inſtructions.

Miſs LEES. I beg pardon, Ma'am; I'll learn to act under nobody but Mr. Frankly. This room is without a carpet; if you will ſtep into the next, ladies, I'll endeavour to oblige you.

Shall I not be environed, diſtraught——

This way, Ladies.

Lady RACH. Pray, Madam, ſhew us the way.

[*Exeunt Miſs* LEES *and Lady* RACH.

Mrs. BEL. I'll prolong this mummery as much as poſſible, in hopes the manager may come. Lye ſtill, poor fluttering heart! it cannot be the lord of all your wiſhes! it cannot ſurely be your ador'd Belville! [*Exit.*

Re-enter

Re-enter Miss Leeson.

Miss LEES. Hav'n't I left my Romeo and Juliet here? O yes, there it is.

Enter Belville.

BEL. ———— *O, were those eyes in heav'n,*
They'd thro' the starry regions stream so bright,
That birds wou'd sing, and think it was the morn!

Miss LEES. Ah, my dear Mr. Frankly! I am so glad you are come! I was dying to see you.

BEL. Kiss me, my dear;—why didn't you send me word of your intention to come away last night?

Miss LEES. I hadn't time: but as I knew where the lodgings were, I thought I shou'd be able to find you by a note to the coffee-house I always directed to.

BEL. Kiss me again, my little sparkler!

Miss LEES. Nay, I won't be kiss'd in this manner; for tho' I am going on the stage, I intend to have some regard for my character. But, ha, ha, ha, I am glad you are come now: I have company above stairs.

BEL. Company! that's unlucky at this time, for I wanted to make you intirely easy about your character. *(aside.)* And pray, my dear, who is your company? You know we must be very cautious for fear of your relations.

Miss LEES. O, they are only ladies.—But one of them is the most beautiful creature in the world!

BEL. The devil she is!

Miss LEES. *An earth-treading star, that makes dim heav'ns light.*

BEL. Zounds! I'll take a peep at the star, who knows but I may have an opportunity of making another actress. *(aside.*

Miss LEES. Come, charmer! charmer!

BEL. ———————— *Wer't thou as far*
As that vast shore, wash'd by the farthest sea,
I wou'd adventure for such merchandize.

F 2

Now let's see what fortune has sent us above stairs.
[Exeunt.

SCENE *changes to a Dining-room at Miss* LEESON'S.

Mrs. BELVILLE *and Lady* RACHEL *discover'd.*

Mrs. BEL. This is a most ignorant young creature, Lady Rachel.

Lady RACH. Why I think she is—did you observe how she slighted my offer of instructing her?

Enter Miss LEESON.

Miss LEES. Ladies!—ladies!—here he is! here is Mr. Frankly!

Enter Belville, *bowing very low, not seeing the Ladies.*

BEL. Ladies, your most obedient.

Mrs. BEL. Let me, if possible, recollect myself—Sir, your most obedient humble servant.

BEL. Zounds! let me out of the house.

Lady RACH. What do I see!

Miss LEES. You seem, ladies, to know this gentleman?

Mrs. BEL. *(taking hold of him)* You shan't go renegade—You laugh'd at my credulity this morning, and I must now laugh at your embarassment.

BEL. What a kind thing it would be in any body to blow out my stupid brains?

Lady RACH. I'll mark this down for an incident in my comedy.

Miss LEES. What do you hang your head for Mr. Frankley?

BEL.

BEL. Be so good as to ask that lady, my dear.—— The Devil has been long in my debt, and now he pays me home with a witness.

Mrs. BEL. What a cruel thing it is to let Mrs. Tempest out, my love, without somebody to take care of her!

Miss LEES. What, do you know Mrs. Tempest, madam?

Mrs. BEL. Yes, my dear;——and I am pretty well acquainted with this gentleman.

Miss LEES. What isn't this gentleman the manager of a play-house in Ireland?

BEL. The curtain is almost dropt my dear; the farce is nearly over, and you'll be speedily acquainted with the catastrophe.

Enter Mrs. TEMPEST.

Mrs. TEMP. Yes, Sir, the curtain is almost dropt: I have had spies to watch your haunts, and the catastrophe ends in your detection.——Come, you abandon'd slut,——

Miss LEES. And have I elop'd after all, without being brought upon the stage?

Mrs TEMP. I don't know that you would be brought upon the stage; but I am sure you were near being brought upon the town. I hope, madam, for the future, you'll set me down a mad-woman.

[*to Mrs. Belville.*

Mrs. BEL. Mr. Belvill, you'll make my apologies to this lady, and acknowledge that I think her perfectly in her senses.

BEL. I wish that I had intirely lost mine.

Lady RACH. *(Writing)* *I wish that I had entirely lost mine.* A very natural wish, in such a situation.

Mrs. TEM. Come, you audacious minx, come away. You shall be sent into Yorkshire this very evening; and see what your poor mother will say to you, hussey.

Miss

Miss LEES. I will go on the stage, if I die for't; and 'tis some comfort there's a play-house at York.
           [*Exit Mrs.* Tempest *and Miss* Leeson.

BEL. Nancy, I am so asham'd, so humbled, and so penitent, that if you knew what passes here, I am sure you wou'd forgive me.

Mrs. BEL. My love, tho' I cannot say I rejoice in your infidelity, yet, believe me, I pity your distress: let us therefore think no more of this.

Lady RACH. *(Writing.) And think no more of this.* ——This conduct is new in a wife, and very dramatic.

BEL. Where, my angel, have you acquired so many requisites to charm with?

Mrs. BEL. In your society, my dear; and believe me ——that a wife may be as true a friend as any bottle companion upon earth, tho' she can neither get merry with you over night, nor blow out your brains about some foolish quarrel in the morning.

BEL. If wives knew the omnipotence of virtue, where she wears a smile upon her face, they'd all follow your bewitching example, and make a faithless husband quite an incredible character.

Lady RACH. *Quite an incredible character!* —— Let me set down that. *(writing.)*   [*Exeunt.*

SCENE *changes to General* SAVAGE's.

Enter General and Captain.

GEN. Yes, Horace, I have been just visiting at Belvill's.

CAPT. You found nobody at home, but Miss Walsingham?

GEN. No, but I'd a long conversation with her, and upon a very interesting subject.

CAPT. 'Tis as I guess'd.   [*aside.*

GEN.

GEN. She is a most amiable creature, Horace.
CAPT. So she is, Sir, and will make any man happy that marries her.
GEN. I am glad you think so.
CAPT. He's glad I think so!——'tis plain,—but I must leave every thing to himself, and seem wholly passive in the affair. [*aside.*
GEN. A married life after all, Horace, I am now convinced is the most happy, as well as the most reputable.
CAPT. It is indeed, Sir.
GEN. Then perhaps you wou'd have no objection to be married, if I offered you as agreeable a young woman as Miss Walsingham.
CAPT. 'Twou'd be my first pride on every occasion, Sir, to pay an implicit obedience to your commands.
GEN. That's sensibly said, Horace, and obligingly said; prepare yourself therefore for an introduction to the lady in the morning.
CAPT. Is the lady prepar'd to receive me, Sir?
GEN. O yes; and you can't think how highly delighted Miss Walsingham appeared, when I acquainted her with my resolution on the subject.
CAPT. She's all goodness!
GEN. The more I know her, the more I am charm'd with her; I must not be explicit with him yet, for fear my secret should get wind, and reach the ears of the enemy. [*aside.*
GEN. I propose, Horace, that you should be married immediately.
CAPT. The sooner the better, Sir, I have no will but your's.
GEN. (*Shaking hands with him,*) By the memory of Malbro', you are a most excellent boy!——But what do you think? Miss Walsingham insists upon naming the day.

CAPT.

CAPT. And welcome, Sir; I am sure she won't make it a distant one.

GEN. O she said, that nothing in her power shou'd be wanting to make you happy.

CAPT. I am sure of that, Sir.

GEN. [*A loud knocking*] Zounds, Horace! here's the disgrace and punishment of my life: Let's avoid her as we would a fever in the camp.

CAPT. Come to the library, and I'll tell you how whimsically she was treated this morning at Belville's.

GEN. Death and the devil! make haste. O I must laugh at marriage, and be curst to me! But I am providing, Horace, against your falling into my error.

CAPT. I am eternally indebted to you, Sir.

[*Exeunt.*

SCENE, BELVILLE's *House.*

Enter Mrs. Belville *and Lady* Rachel.

Lady RACH. Nay, Mrs. Belville, I have no patience, you act quite unnaturally.

Mrs. BEL. What! because I am unwilling to be miserable?

Lady RACH. This new instance of Mr. Belville's infidelity——This attempt to seduce Miss Walsingham, which your woman overheard, is unpardonable!

Mrs. BEL. I don't say but that I am strongly wounded by his irregularities. Yet if Mr. Belville is unhappily a rover, I wou'd much rather that he should have twenty mistresses than one.

Lady RACH. You astonish me!

Mrs. BEL. Why, don't you know, my dear madam, that while he is divided amidst a variety of objects, 'tis impossible for him to have a serious attachment?

Lady

Lady RACH. Lord, Mrs. Belville! how can you speak with so much composure! a virtuous woman should be always outrageous upon such an occasion as this.

Mrs. BEL. What, and weary the innocent sun and moon from the firmament, like a despairing princess in a tragedy—No—no—Lady Rachel, 'tis bad enough to be indifferent to the man I love, without studying to excite his aversion.

Lady RACH. How glad I am that Miss Walsingham made him so heartily asham'd of himself: Lord, these young men are so full of levity: Give me a husband of Mr. Torrington's age, say I.

Mrs. BEL. And give me a husband of Mr. Belville's, say I, with all his follies: However, Lady Rachel, I am pretty well satisfied that my conduct at Miss Leeson's will have a proper effect upon Mr. Belville's generosity, and put an entire end to his galantries for the future.

Lady RACH. Don't deceive yourself, my dear.---The gods in the shilling gallery would sooner give up Roast Beef, or go without an epilogue on the first night of a new piece.

Mrs. BEL. Why should you think so of such a man as Mr. Belville?

Lady RACH. Because Mr. Belville is a man: However, if you dare run the risque---we will try the sincerity of his reformation.

Mrs. BEL. If I dare run the risque! I would stake my soul upon his honour.

Lady RACH. Then your poor soul would be in a very terrible situation.

Mrs. BEL. By what test can we prove his sincerity?

Lady RACH. By a very simple one. You know I write so like Miss Walsingham, that our hands are scarcely known asunder.

Mrs. BEL. Well——

Lady RACH. Why then let me write to him as from her—

Mrs. BEL. If I did not think it would look like a doubt of his honour—

Lady RACH. Poh! dare you proceed upon my plan?—

Mrs. BEL. Most confidently: Come to my dressing-room, where you'll find every thing ready for writing, and then you may explain your scheme more particularly.

Lady RACH. I'll attend you, but I am really sorry, my dear, for the love of propriety, to see you so calm under the perfidy of your husband; you should be quite wretched—indeed you should. [*Ex.*

SCENE, *the Temple.*

Enter Leeson.

LEES. The hell-hounds are after me.

Enter Connolly, *at the opposite side.*

Fly, open the chambers this moment, the bailiffs are in sight.

CON. Faith and that I will; but it will be of no use to fly a step, if I hav'n't the key.

LEES. Zounds! did not you lock the door?

CON. Yes; but I believe I left the key on the inside: However, I see no more than three people, and think we could beat them to their hearts content in three minutes.

LEES. What! and fly in the face of the law?

CON. To be sure you have a great regard for the law, when you are going to fight a duel!

LEES. S'death! is this a time to talk? Stay here, and throw every possible impediment in the way of these execrable rascals. (*going.*)

CON.

Con. Holloa! honey, come back: These execrable rascals are very worthy people, I fancy, for they are quietly turning down the next court.

Lees. Their appearance alarm'd me beyond measure.

Con. O you shou'dn't judge by outside shew, my dear; for there is no being a complete rogue, without the appearance of an honest man

Lees. Circumstanced as I am at present, every thing terrifies me; for should I be arrested, the consequence would possibly be fatal, both to my honour and my love.---Belville would proclaim me publicly a coward; and Emily set me down as a base, a mercenary adventurer, who was solely attracted by her fortune.

Con. Why faith, honey, like yourself, they might be apt to judge by appearances.

Lees. O, Connolly, a man of spirit should learn prudence from his very pride, and consider every unnecessary debt he contracts as a wanton diminution of his character! the moment he makes another his creditor---he makes himself a slave! He runs the hazard of insults, which he never can resent, and of disgraces which are seldom to be mitigated! He incurs the danger of being dragg'd, like the vilest felon to the felon's prison! and, such is the depravity of the world, that guilt is even more likely to meet with advocates, than misfortune! [*Exit Leeson.*

Con. Musha, long life to you, ould Shillala!---I wish I had any thing besides my carcase to venture for you, for that's nothing; yet you are as welcome to it as the flowers in May. Poor lad! I don't wonder that he is so much afraid of a prison, for to be sure it is a blessed place to live in; and a blessed law it must be, which coops a man up from every chance of getting money, by way of making him pay his debts---But now let my thick skull consider, if there is any method of preventing this infernal duel. Suppose I have him bound

bound over to the pace! No, that will never do---it would be a shameful thing for a gintleman to keep the pace! Besides, I muft appear in the bufinefs, and people may think, from my connexion with him, that he has not honour enough to throw away his life: Suppofe I go another way to work, and fend an anonymous letter about the affair to Mrs. Belville: They fay, though fhe is a woman of fafhion, that no creter upon earth can be fonder of her hufband. Surely the good genius of Ireland put this fcheme into my head---I'll about it this minute; and if there's only one of them kept from the field, I don't think that the other can be much hurt, when there will be no body to fight with him. [*Exit.*

SCENE, *changes to Capt.* SAVAGE's *Lodgings.*

Enter Captain SAVAGE *and* BELVILLE.

CAPT. Why, faith, Belville, your detection, and fo speedily too, after all the pretended fanctity of the morning, muft have thrown you into a moft humiliating fituation.

BEL. Into the moft diftreffing you can imagine: had my wife rav'd at my falfehood, in the cuftomary manner, I cou'd have brazen'd it out pretty tollerably; but the angel-like fweetnefs, with which fhe bore the mortifying difcovery, planted daggers in my bofom, and made me at that time wifh her the verieft vixen in the whole creation.

CAPT. Yet, the fuffering forbearance of a wife, is a quality for which fhe is feldom allow'd her merit; we think it her duty to put up with our falfehood, and imagine ourfelves exceedingly generous in the main, if we practife no other method of breaking her heart.

BEL. Morftrous! monftrous! from this moment
I bid

I bid an everlasting adieu to my vices: the generosity of my dear girl——

Enter a Servant to BELVILLE.

SERV. Here's a letter, Sir, which Mr. Spruce has brought you.

BEL. Give me leave, Savage.—Zounds! what an industrious devil the father of darkness is, when the moment a man determines upon a good action, he sends such a thing as this, to stagger his resolution.

CAPT. What have you got there?

BEL. You shall know presently. Will you let Spruce come in.

CAPT. Where have you acquir'd all this ceremony?

BEL. Bid Spruce come in.

SERV. Yes, Sir. [*Exit.*

CAPT. Is that another challenge?

BEL. 'Tis upon my soul, but it came from a beautiful enemy, and dares me to give a meeting to Miss Walsingham.

CAPT. How!

Enter SPRUCE.

BEL. Pray, Spruce, who gave you this letter?

SPRUCE. Miss Walsingham's woman, Sir: she said it was about very particular business, and therefore I wou'dn't trust it by any of the footmen.

CAPT. O, damn your diligence. (*aside.*)

BEL. You may go home, Spruce.

SPRUCE. (*Looking significantly at his Master.*) Is there no answer necessary, Sir.

BEL. I shall call at home myself, and give the necessary answer,

SPRUCE. (*Aside.*) What can be the matter with him all of a sudden, that he is so cold upon the scent of wickedness? [*Exit.*

CAPT. And what answer do you propose making to it, Belville? BEL.

Bel. Read the letter, and then tell me what I shou'd do.---You know Miss Walsingham's hand.

Capt. O, perfectly!---This is not---yes, it is her hand!---I have too many curst occasions to know it.
(aside.)

Bel. What are you a muttering about?---Read the letter.

Capt. *If you are not entirely discouraged, by our last conversation, from renewing the subject which* then *gave offence*———

Bel. *Which then gave offence.*---You see, Savage, that it is not offensive any longer.

Capt. Sdeath! you put me out.---*you may at the masquerade, this evening*———

Bel. You remember how earnest she was for the masquerade party.

Capt. Yes, yes, I remember it well:---and I remember, also, how hurt she was this morning, about the affair of Miss Leeson. *(aside.)*———*have an opportunity of entertaining me*———O the strumpet! *(aside.)*

Bel. But mind the cunning with which she signs the note, for fear it shou'd by any accident fall into improper hands.

Capt. Ay, and you put it into very proper hands. *(aside.)* *I shall be in the blue domino.*---The signature is---... You know who.

Bel. Yes, *you know who.*

Capt. May be, however, she has only written this to try you.

Bel. To try me, for what purpose? But if you read a certain postcript there, I fancy you'll be of a different opinion.

Capt. *If Mr. Belville has any house of character to retire to, it wou'd be most agreeable, as there cou'd be no fear of interruption.*

Bel. What do you say now?---Can you recommend

mend me to any house of character, where we shall be free from interruption.

CAPT. O, curse her house of character! *(aside)* But surely, Belville, after your late determin'd resolution to reform---

BEL. Zounds! I forgot that.

CAPT. After the unexampled sweetness of your wife's behaviour---

BEL. Don't go on, Savage: There is something here *(putting his hand upon his bosom)* which feels already not a little aukwardly.

CAPT. And can you still persist?

BEL. I am afraid to answer your question.

CAPT. Where the plague are you flying?

BEL. From the justice of your censure, Horace; my own is sufficiently severe; yet I see that I shall be a rascal again, in spite of my teeth; and good advice is only thrown away upon so incorrigible a libertine.

[*Exit.*

CAPT. *(alone)* So then this diamond of mine proves a counterfeit after all, and I am really the veriest wretch existing at the moment in which I conceiv'd myself the peculiar favourite of fortune. O the cursed, cursed sex! I'll see her once more to upbraid her with her falsehood, then acquaint my father with her perfidy, to justify my breaking off the marriage, and tear her from my thoughts for ever.

Enter a Servant.

SERV. Sir! Sir! Sir!—

CAPT. Sir, Sir, Sir,—What the devil's the matter with the booby?

SERV. Miss Walsingham, Sir!

CAPT. Ah! what of her?

SERV. Was this moment overturn'd at Mr. Belville's door, and John tells me carried in a fit into the house.

CAPT.

CAPT. Ha! let me fly to her affiftance. [*Exit.*
SERV. *Ha let me fly to her affiftance*—O, are you thereabouts. [*Exit.*

SCENE *changes to Mr.* BELVILLE'*s.*

Enter Mrs. Belville, *Mifs* Walfingham *and Lady* Rachel Mildew.

Mrs. BEL. But are you indeed recover'd my dear?
Mifs WAL. Perfectly my dear,—I wasn't in the leaft hurt, tho' greatly terrified, when the two fools of coachmen contended for the honour of being firft, and drove the carriages together with a violence incredible.

Lady RACH. I fincerely rejoice at your efcape; and now Mrs. Belville, as you promifed to choofe a drefs for me if I went in your party to the mafquerade this evening, can you fpare a quarter of an hour to Taviftock-Street?

Mrs. BEL. I am loth to leave Mifs Walfingham alone, Lady Rachel, fo foon after her fright.

Mifs WAL Nay, I infift that you don't ftay at home upon my account; and Lady Rachel's company to the mafquerade is a pleafure I have fuch an intereft in, that I beg you won't delay a moment to oblige her.

Mrs. BEL. Well, then I attend your ladyfhip.

Lady RACH. You are very good; and fo is Mifs Walfingham. [*Exit.*

Mifs WAL. I wonder Captain Savage ftays away fo long! where can he be all this time?—I die with impatience to tell him of my happy interview with the General.

Enter a Servant.

SERV. Captain Savage, madam.

Miss WAL. Shew him in. [*Exit Serv.*] How he must rejoice to find his conjectures so fortunately realiz'd.

Enter Captain Savage.

CAPT. So, madam, you have just escap'd a sad accident.

Miss WAL. And by that agreeable tone and countenance, one would almost imagine you were very sorry for my escape.

CAPT. People, madam, who doubt the kindness of others, are generally conscious of some defect in themselves.

Miss WAL. Don't madam me, with this accent of indifference. What has put you out of humour?

CAPT. Nothing.

Miss WAL. Are you indispos'd?

CAPT. The Crocodile! the Crocodile! [*aside.*

Miss WAL. Do you go to the masquerade to night?

CAPT. No, but you do.

Miss WAL. Why not? come, don't be ill-natur'd, I'm not your wife yet.

CAPT. Nor ever will be, I promise you.

Miss WAL. What is the meaning of this very whimsical behaviour?

CAPT. The settled composure of her impudence is intolerable. (*aside.*) Madam, Madam, how have I deserv'd this usage?

Miss WAL. Nay, Sir, Sir, how have I deserved it, if you go to that?

CAPT. The letter, madam!——the letter!

Miss WAL. What letter?

CAPT. Your letter, inviting a gallant from the masquerade to a house of character, madam!——What, you appear surpriz'd?

Miss WAL. Well I may, at so shameless an aspersion.

CAPT. Madam, madam, I have seen your letter!

Your new lover cou'dn't keep your secret a moment. But I have nothing to do with you,—and only come to declare my reasons for renouncing you everlastingly!

Enter Servant.

SERV. General Savage, madam.

Miss WAL. Shew him up. [*Exit Serv.*] I am glad he is come, Sir; inform him of your resolution to break off the match, and let there be an end of every thing between us.

Enter General Savage.

GEN. The news of your accident reach'd me but this moment, madam,——or I shou'd have posted much sooner to reconnoitre your situation. My aid de camp, however, has not been inattentive I see, and I dare say his diligence will not be the least lessen'd, when he knows his obligations to you.

CAPT. O, Sir, I am perfectly sensible of my obligations; and the consciousness of them, was one motive of my coming here.

GEN. Then you have made your acknowledgements to miss Walsingham I hope.

Miss WAL. He has indeed, General, said a great deal more than was necessary.

GEN. That opinion proceeds from the liberality of your temper; for 'tis impossible he can ever say enough of your goodness.

CAPT. So it is; if you knew but all, Sir.

GEN. Why who can know more of the matter than myself?

Miss WAL. This gentleman, it seems, has something, General Savage, very necessary for your information.

GEN. How's this?

CAPT. Nay, Sir, I only say, that for some particular reasons, which I shall communicate to you at a

more

more proper time; I muſt beg leave to decline the lady whoſe hand you kindly intended for me this morning.

GEN. O you muſt!---Why then I hope you decline at the ſame time, all pretenſions to every ſhilling of my fortune. It is not in my power to make you fight, you paltroon, but I can puniſh you for cowardice.

Miſs WAL. Nay, but General, let me interpoſe here. If he can maintain any charge againſt the lady's reputation, 'twould be very hard that he ſhould be diſinherited, for a neceſſary attention to his honour.

CAPT. And if I don't make the charge good, I ſubmit to be diſinherited without murmuring.

GEN. 'Tis falſe as hell! the lady is infinitely too good for you, in every reſpect; and I undervalued her worth, when I thought of her for your wife.

Miſs WAL. I am ſure the lady is much oblig'd to your favourable opinion, Sir.

GEN. Not in the leaſt, Madam; I only do her common juſtice.

CAPT. I cannot bear that you ſhou'd be diſpleas'd a moment, Sir; ſuffer me therefore to render the converſation leſs equivocal, and a few words will explain every thing.

GEN. Sirrah, I'll hear no explanation; ar'n't my orders that you ſhou'd marry?

Miſs WAL. For my ſake hear him, General Savage.

CAPT. Madam, I diſdain every favour that is to be procur'd by your interpoſition. [*Exit.*

Miſs WAL. This matter muſt not be ſuffer'd to proceed farther tho', provokingly, cruelly as the Captain has behav'd. (*aſide.*

GEN. What's that you ſay, my bewitching girl?

Miſs WAL. I ſay that you muſt make it up with the Captain, and the beſt way will be to hear his charge patiently.   GEN.

Gen. I am shock'd at the brutality of the dog; he has no more principle than a suttler, and no more steadiness than a young recruit upon drill. But, you shall have ample satisfaction:——this very day I'll cut him off from a possibility of succeeding to a shilling of my fortune. He shall be as miserable as——

Miss Wal. Dear General, do you think that this wou'd give me any satisfaction?

Gen. How he became acquainted with my design I know not, but I see plainly, that his mutiny proceeds from his aversion to my marrying again.

Miss Wal. To your marrying again, Sir! why shou'd he object to that?

Gen. Why, for fear I should have other children, to be sure.

Miss Wal. Indeed, Sir, it was not from that motive; and, if I can overlook his folly, you may be prevail'd upon to forgive it.

Gen. After what you have seen, justice shou'd make you a little more attentive to your own interest, my lovely girl.

Miss Wal. What at the expence of his?

Gen. In the approaching change of your situation, there may be a family of your own.

Miss Wal. Suppose there shou'd, Sir; won't there be a family of his too?

Gen. I care not what becomes of his family.

Miss Wal. But, pray let me think a little about it, General.

Gen. 'Tis hard, indeed, when I was so desirous of promoting his happiness, that he should throw any thing in the way of mine.

Miss Wal. Recollect, Sir, his offence was wholly confin'd to me.

Gen. Well, my love, and isn't it throwing an obstacle in the way of my happiness, when he abuses you so grosly for your readiness to marry me?

Miss Wal. Sir!——

Gen.

GEN. I see, with all your good nature, that this is a question you cannot rally against.

Miss WAL. It is indeed, Sir.—What will become of me? (*aside.*)

GEN. You seem suddenly disordered, my love?

Miss WAL. Why really, Sir, this affair affects me strongly.

GEN. Well, it is possible, that for your sake, I may not punish him with as much severity as I intended: In about an hour I shall beg leave to beat up your quarters again, with Mr. Torrington; for 'tis necessary I should shew you some proof of my gratitude, since you have been so kindly pleas'd to honour me with a proof of your affection.

Miss WAL. (*aside.*) So, now indeed, we're in a hopeful situation. [*Exeunt.*

ACT IV.

SCENE, *an Apartment at* BELVILLE's.

Enter Mrs. Belville, *and Captain* Savage.

Mrs. BEL. DON'T argue with me, Captain Savage; but consider that I am a wife, and pity my distraction.

CAPT. Dear Madam, there is no occasion to be so much alarm'd; Mr. Belville has very properly determin'd not to fight; he told me so himself, and should have been effectually prevented, if I hadn't known his resolution.

Mrs. BEL. There is no knowing to what extremities he may be provok'd, if he meets Mr. Leeson; I have sent for you, therefore, to beg that you will save him from the possibility, either of exposing himself to any danger, or of doing an injury to his adversary.

CAPT.

CAPT. What would you have me do, Madam?

Mrs. BEL. Fly to Hyde-park, and prevent, if yet possible, his meeting with Mr. Leeson: Do it, I conjure you,—if you'd save me from desperation.

CAPT. Though you have no reason whatever to be apprehensive for his safety, Madam, yet, since you are so very much affected, I'll immediately execute your commands. [*Exit.*

Mrs. BEL. Merciful heaven! where is the generosity, where is the sense, where is the shame of men, to find a pleasure in pursuits, which they cannot remember without the deepest horror; which they cannot follow without the meanest fraud; and which they cannot effect, without consequences the most dreadful? The single word, Pleasure, in a masculine sense, comprehends every thing that is cruel; every thing that is base; and every thing that is desperate: Yet men, in other respects, the noblest of their species, make it the principal business of their lives, and do not hesitate to break in upon the peace of the happiest families, though their own must be necessarily expos'd to destruction.----O Belville! Belville!---my life! my love!--The greatest triumph which a libertine can ever experience, is too despicable to be envied; 'tis at best nothing but a victory over his own humanity; and if he is a husband, he must be dead indeed, if he is not doubly tortured upon the wheel of recollection.

Enter Miss WALSINGHAM *and Lady* RACHEL MILDEW.

Miss WAL. My dear Mrs. Belville, I am extremely unhappy to see you so distress'd.

Lady RACH. Now, I am extremely glad to see her so, for if she wasn't greatly distress'd it wou'd be monstrously unnatural.

Mrs. BEL. O, Matilda!—my husband! my husband! my children! my children!

Miss WAL. Don't weep, my dear! don't weep! pray be comforted, all may end happily. Lady Rachel, beg of her not to cry so.

Lady RACH. Why, you are crying yourself, Miss Walsingham; and tho' I think it out of character to encourage her tears, I can't help keeping you company.

Mrs. BEL. O, why is not some effectual method contriv'd, to prevent this horrible practice of duelling?

Lady RACH. I'll expose it on the stage, since the law now-a-days, kindly leaves the whole cognizance of it to the theatre.

Miss WAL. And yet if the laws against it, were as well enforced as the laws against destroying the game, perhaps it would be equally for the benefit of the kingdom.

Mrs. BEL. No law will ever be effectual till the custom is render'd infamous.----Wives must shriek!----mothers must agonize!---orphans must multiply! unless some blessed hand strips the fascinating glare from honourable murder, and bravely exposes the idol who is worship'd thus in blood. While it is disreputable to obey the laws, we cannot look for reformation :----But if the duellist is once banished from the presence of his sovereign;----if he is for life excluded the confidence of his country;----if a mark of indelible disgrace is stamp'd upon him, the sword of publick justice will be the sole chastiser of wrongs; trifles will not be punish'd with death, and offences really meriting such a punishment, will be reserv'd for the only proper avenger, the common executioner.

Lady RACH. I cou'dn't have express'd myself better on the subject, my dear: but till such a hand as you talk of is found, the best will fall into the error of the times.

Miss WAL. Yes, and butcher each other like madmen, for fear their courage should be suspected by fools.

Mrs. BEL. No news yet from Captain Savage?

Lady RACH. He can't have reach'd Hyde-park yet, my dear.

Miss WAL. Let us lead you to your chamber, my dear; you'll be better there.

Mrs.

Mrs. BEL. Matilda; I muſt be wretched any where; but I'll attend you.

Lady RACH. Thank heav'n; I have no huſband to plunge me into ſuch a ſituation!

Miſs WAL. And, if I thought I cou'd keep my reſolution, I'd determine this moment on living ſingle all the days of my life. Pray don't ſpare my arm, my dear. [*Exeunt.*

SCENE, *Hyde Park.*

Enter BELVILLE.

BEL. I fancy I am rather before the time of appointment; engagements of this kind are the only ones, in which, now-a-days, people pretend, to any punctuality:---a man is allow'd half an hours law to dinner, but a thruſt through the body muſt be given within a ſecond of the clock.

Enter Leeſon.

LEES. Your ſervant, Sir.---Your name I ſuppoſe is Belville?

BEL. Your ſuppoſition is very right, Sir; and I fancy I am not much in the wrong, when I ſuppoſe your name to be Leeſon.

LEES. It is, Sir; I am ſorry I ſhou'd keep you here a moment.

BEL. I am very ſorry, Sir, you ſhou'd bring me here at all.

LEES. I regret the occaſion, be aſſured, Sir; but 'tis not now a time for talking, we muſt proceed to action.

BEL. And yet talking is all the action I ſhall proceed to, depend upon it.

LEES. What do you mean, Sir? Where are your piſtols?

BEL. Where I intend they ſhall remain till my next journey into the country, very quietly over the chimney in my dreſſing room.

LEES. You treat this matter with too much levity, Mr. Belville; take your choice of mine, Sir.

BEL.

Bel. I'd rather take them both, if you please, for then no mischief shall be done with either of them.

Lees. Sir, this trifling is adding insult to injury; and shall be resented accordingly. Didn't you come here to give me satisfaction?

Bel. Yes, every satisfaction in my power.

Lees. Take one of these pistols then.

Bel. Come, Mr. Leeson, your bravery will not at all be lessen'd by the exercise of a little understanding: If nothing less than my life can atone for the injury I have unconsciously done you, fire at me instantly, but don't be offended because I decline to do you an additional wrong.

Lees. S'death, Sir, do you think I come here with an intention to murder?

Bel. You come to arm the guilty against the innocent, Sir; and that, in my opinion, is the most atrocious intention of murder.

Lees. How's this?---

Bel. Look'e, Mr. Leeson, there's your pistol *(throws it on the ground)* I have already acted very wrongly with respect to your sister, but, Sir, I have some character (though perhaps little enough) to maintain, and I will not do a still worse action, in raising my hand against your life.

Lees. This hypocritical cant of cowardice, Sir, is too palpable to disarm my resentment; though I held you to be a man of profligate principles, I nevertheless consider'd you as a man of courage; but, if you hesitate a moment longer, by heaven, I'll chastise you on the spot. *(Draws.)*

Bel. I must defend my life; though if it did not look like timidity, I would inform you---*(they fight, Leeson is disarmed)*---Mr. Leeson, there is your sword again.

Lees. Strike it through my bosom, Sir;---I don't desire to out-live this instant.

Bel. I hope, my dear Sir, that you will long live happy

happy—as your sister, tho' to my shame I can claim no merit on that account, is recovered unpolluted, by her family; but let me beg that you will now see the folly of decisions by the sword, when success is not fortunately chain'd to the side of justice: Before I leave you, receive my sincerest apologies for the injuries I have done you; and, be assured, no occurrence will ever give me greater pleasure, than an opportunity of serving you, if, after what is past, you shall at any time condescend to use me as a friend. [*Ex.*

LEES. Very well---very well---very well.

Enter Connolly.

LEES. What, you have been within hearing, I suppose?
CON. You may say that.

LEES. And isn't this very fine?

CON. Why I can't say much as to the finery of it, Sir, but it is certainly very foolish.

LEES. And so this is my satisfaction after all!

CON. Yes, and pretty satisfaction it is. When Mr. Belville did you but one injury, he was the greatest villain in the world; but now that he has done you two, in drawing his sword upon you, I suppose he is a very worthy gentleman

LEES. To be foil'd, baffled, disappointed in my revenge!--What tho' my sister is by accident unstain'd, his intentions are as criminal, as if her ruin was actually perpetrated; there is no possibility of enduring the reflection!---I wish not for the blood of my enemy, but I would at least have the credit of giving him life.

CON. Arrah, my dear, if you had any regard for the life of your enemy, you shou'dn't put him in the way of death.

LEES. No more of these reflections, my dear Connolly; my own feelings are painful enough. Will you be so good as to take these damn'd pistols, and come with me to the coach?

CON. Troth and that I will; but don't make yourself

self uneasy; consider that you have done every thing which honour required at yous hands.

Lees. I hope so.

Con. Why you know so: You have broke the laws of heaven and earth, as nobly as the first lord in the land, and you have convinc'd the world, that where any body has done your family one injury, you have courage enough to do it another yourself, by hazarding your life.

Lees. Those, Connolly, who would live reputably in any country, must regulate their conduct in many cases by its very prejudices.----Custom, with respect to duelling, is a tyrant, whose despotism no body ventures to attack, tho' every body detests its cruelty.

Con. I didn't imagine that a tyrant of any kind would, be tolerated in England. But where do you think of going now? For chambers, you know, are at present most delightfully dangerous.

Lees. I shall go to Mrs. Crayon's.

Con. What the gentlewoman that paints all manner of colours in red chalk?

Lees. Yes, where I first became acquainted with Emily.

Con. And where the sweet creature has met you two or three times under pretence of sitting for her picture.

Lees. Mrs. Crayons will, I dare say, oblige me in this exigency with an apartment for a few days; but come, Connolly, we have no time to lose, tho' if you had any prudence, you would abandon me in my present situation.

Con. Ah, Sir, is this your opinion of my friendship? Do you think that any thing can ever give me half so much pleasure in serving you, as seeing you surrounded by misfortunes. [*Exeunt.*

The Scene changes to an Apartment at Belville's.

Enter General Savage, Torrington, *and* Spruce.

Spruce. Miss Walsingham will wait on you immediately, gentlemen.

GEN. Very well.

SPRUCE. (*aside*) What can old Holifernes want so continually with Miss Walsingham? [*Exit*

GEN. When I bring this sweet mild creature home, I shall be able to break her spirit to my own wishes—I'll inure her to proper discipline from the first moment, and make her tremble at the very thought of mutiny.

TOR. Ah, General, you are wonderfully brave, when you know the meekness of your adversary.

GEN. Envy, Torrington——stark, staring envy: few fellows, on the borders of fifty, have so much reason as myself, to boast of a blooming young woman's partiality.

TOR. On the borders of fifty, man!—beyond the confines of threescore.

GEN. The more reason I have to boast of my victory then; but don't grumble at my triumph, you shall have a kiss of the bride, let that content you, Torrington.

Enter Miss Walsingham.

MISS WAL. Gentlemen, your most obedient: General, I intended writing to you about a trifling mistake; but poor Mrs. Belville has been so very ill, that I cou'dn't find an opportunity.

GEN. I am very sorry for Mrs. Belville's illness, but I am happy, Madam, to be personally in the way of receiving your commands, and I wait upon you with Mr. Torrington, to talk about a marriage settlement.

MISS WAL. Heavens! how shall I undeceive him?
(*aside.*

TOR. 'Tis rather an aukward business, Miss Walsingham, to trouble you upon; but as the General wishes that the affair may be as private as possible, he thought it better to speak to yourself, than to treat with any other person.

GEN. Yes, my lovely girl; and to convince you,
that

that I intend to carry on an honourable war, not to pillage like a free-booter, Mr. Torrington will be a trustee.

Miss WAL. I am infinitely oblig'd to your intention, but there's no necessity to talk about any settlement—for—

GEN. Pardon me, Madam,—pardon me, there is—besides, I have determin'd that there shall be one, and what I once determine is absolute.—A tolerable hint for her own behaviour, when I have married her, Torrington. *(aside to Tor.)*

Miss WAL. I must not shock him before Mr. Torrington *(aside)*. General Savage, will you give me leave to speak a few words in private to you.

GEN. There is no occasion for founding a retreat, Madam; Mr. Torrington is acquainted with the whole business, and I am determin'd, for your sake, that nothing sha'l be done without him.

TOR. I can have no objection to your hearing the lady ex parte, General.

Miss WAL. What I have to say, Sir, is of a very particular nature.

TOR. *(rising)* I'll leave the room then.

GEN. *(opposing him)* You shan't leave the room, Torrington. Miss Walsingham shall have a specimen of my command, even before marriage, and you shall see, that every woman is not to bully me out of my determination. *(aside to Tor.)*

Miss WAL. Well, General, you must have your own way.

GEN. *(to Tor.)* Don't you see that it's only fighting the battle stoutly at first, with one of these gentle creatures?

TOR. *(significantly)* Ah, General!

GEN. I own, Madam, your situation is a distressing one; let us sit down—let us sit down—

Miss WAL. It is unspeakably distressing indeed, Sir.

TOR. Distressing however as it may be; we must proceed

ceed to issue, Madam; the General proposes your jointure to be 1000 l. a year.

Miss WAL. General Savage!

GEN. You think this too little, perhaps?

Miss WAL. I can't think of any jointure, Sir.

TOR. Why to be sure, a jointure it at best but a melancholly possession, for it must be purchased by the loss of the husband you love.

Miss WAL. Pray don't name it, Mr. Torrington.

GEN. (*kissing her hand*) A thousand thanks to you, my lovely girl.

Miss WAL. For heaven's sake, let go my hand.

GEN. I shall be mad 'till it gives me legal possession of the town.

Miss WAL. Gentlemen—General----Mr. Torrington---I beg you'll hear me.

GEN. By all means, my adorable creature; I can never have too many proofs of your disinterested affection.

Miss WAL. There is a capital mistake in this whole affair---I am sinking under a load of distress.

GEN. Your confusion makes you look charmingly though.

Miss WAL. There is no occasion to talk of jointures or marriages to me; I am not going to be married.

TOR. What's this?

Miss WAL. Nor have I an idea in nature, however enviable I think the honour, of being your wife, Sir.

GEN. Madam!

TOR. Why here's a demur!

Miss WAL. I am afraid, Sir, that in our conversation this morning, my confusion arising from the particularity of the subject, has led you into a material misconception.

GEN. I am thunderstruck, madam! I cou'dn't mistake my ground.

TOR. As clear a *nol: pros:* as ever was issued by an attorney general.

GEN. Surely you can't forget, that at the first word you hung out a flag of truce, told me even that

that I had a previous friend in the fort, and didn't so much as hint at a single article of capitulation?

Tor. Now for the rejoinder to this replication.

Miss Wal. All this is unquestionably true, General, and perhaps a good deal more; but in reality my confusion before you on this subject to day, was such, that I scarcely knew what I said; I was dying with distress, and at this moment am very little better;—permit me to retire, General Savage, and only suffer me to add, that tho' I think myself highly flatter'd by your addresses, it is impossible for me ever to receive them. Lord! Lord! I am glad its over in any manner. [*Ex.*

Tor. Why, we are a little out in this matter, General; the judge has decided against us, when we imagin'd ourselves sure of the cause.

Gen. The gates shut in my teeth, just as I expected the keys from the governor.

Tor. I am disappointed myself, man; I shan't have a kiss of the bride.

Gen. At my time of life too!

Tor. I said from the first you were too old for her.

Gen. Zounds to fancy myself sure of her, and to triumph upon a certainty of victory.

Tor. Ay, and to kiss her hand in a rapturous return for her tenderness to you :—let me advise you never to kiss before folks, as long as you live again.

Gen. Don't distract me, Torrington! a joke, where a friend has the misfortune to lose the battle, is a downright inhumanity.

Tor. You told me that your son had accus'd her of something that you would not hear; suppose we call at his lodgings, he perhaps, as an *amicus-curiæ*, may be able to give us a little information.

Gen. Thank you for the thought;—But keep your finger more than ever upon you lips, dear Torrington. You know how I dread the danger of ridicule, and it wou'd be too much, not only to be thrash'd out of the field, but to be laugh'd at into the bargain.

Tor.

Tor. I thought when you made a presentment of your sweet person to Miss Walsingham, that the bill wou'd be return'd ignoramus. [*Exeunt.*

SCENE, BELVILLE'S.

Mrs. BELVILLE *and Lady* RACHEL MILDEW, *discovered on a Sopha.*

Lady RACH. You heard what Captain Savage said?

Mrs. BEL. I would flatter myself, but my heart will not suffer it; the Park might be too full for the horrid purpose, and perhaps they are gone to decide the quarrel in some other place.

Lady RACH. The Captain enquir'd of numbers in the Park without hearing a syllable of them, and is therefore positive that they are parted without doing any mischief.

Mrs. BEL. I am, nevertheless, torn by a thousand apprehensions, and my fancy, with a gloomy kind of fondness, fastens on the most deadly. This very morning, I exultingly numbered myself in the catalogue of the happiest wives.—Perhaps I am a wife no longer;—perhaps, my little innocents, your unhappy father is at this moment breathing his last sigh, and wishing, O, how vainly! that he had not prefer'd a guilty pleasure to his own life, to my eternal peace of mind, and your felicity!

Enter SPRUCE.

SPRUCE. Madam! madam! my master! my master!

Mrs. BEL. Is he safe?

Enter BELVILLE.

BEL. My love!

Mrs. BEL. O Mr. Belville! (*faints.*

BEL. Assistance, quick!

Lady RACH. There she revives.

BEL. The angel-softness! how this rends my heart?

Mrs. BEL. O, Mr. Belville, if you cou'd conceive
the

the agonies I have endur'd, you would avoid the poffibility of another quarrel as long as you liv'd, out of common humanity.

Bel. My dearest creature, spare these tender reproaches; you know not how sufficiently I am punish'd to see you thus miserable.

Lady Rach. That's pleasant indeed, when you have yourself deliberately loaded her with affliction.

Bel. Pray, pray Lady Rachel, have a little mercy: Your poor humble servant has been a very naughty boy,--but if you only forgive him this single time, he will never more deserve the rod of correction.

Mrs. Bel. Since you are return'd safe, I am happy. Excuse these foolish tears, they gush in spite of me.

Bel. How contemptible do they render me, my love!

Lady Rach. Come, my dear, you must turn your mind from this gloomy subject.—Suppose we step up stairs and communicate our pleasure to Miss Walsingham?

Mrs. Bel. With all my heart. Adieu, recreant!

[*Exeunt Mrs.* Bel. *and Lady* Rach.

Bel. I don't deserve such a woman, I don't deserve her.—Yet, I believe I am the first husband, that ever found fault with a wife, for having too much goodness.

Enter Spruce.

What's the matter?

Spruce. Your sister——

Bel. What of my sister?

Spruce. Sir, is elop'd.

Bel. My sister!

Spruce. There is a letter left, Sir, in which she says, that her motive was a dislike to a match with Captain Savage, as she has plac'd her affections unalterably on another gentleman.

Bel. Death and damnation!

Spruce. Mrs. Moreland, your mother, is in the greatest distress, Sir, and begs you will immediately go with the servant that brought the message; for he observing the young lady's maid carrying some bundles out, a little suspiciously, thought there must be some scheme going on, and dogg'd a hackney coach, in which Miss Morland went off, to the very house where it set her down.

BEL. Bring me to the servant, instantly;—but don't let a syllable of this matter reach my wife's ears, her spirits are already too mnch agitated. [*Exit.*

SPRUCE. Zounds! we shall be paid home, for the tricks we have play'd in other families. [*Exit.*

Scene changes to Capt. SAVAGE's *Lodgings.*

Enter Captain SAVAGE.

CAPT. The vehemence of my resentment against this abandon'd woman has certainly led me too far. I shou'dn't have acquainted her with my discovery of her baseness;—no, if I had acted properly, I should have conceal'd all knowledge of the transaction 'till the very moment of her guilt, and then burst upon her when she was solacing with her paramour, in all the fulness of security. Now, if she should either alter her mind, with respect to going to the masquerade, or go in a different habit to elude my observation, I not only lose the opportunity of exposing her, but give her time to plan some plausible excuse for her infamous letter to Belville.

Enter a Servant.

SER. General Savage, and Mr. Torrington, Sir.

CAPT. You blockhead, why did you let them wait a moment? What can be the meaning of this visit? [*Ex. Servant.*

Enter General SAVAGE, *and* TORRINGTON.

GEN. I come, Horace, to talk to you about Miss Walsingham.

CAPT

Capt. She's the most worthless woman existing, Sir: I can convince you of it.

Gen. I have already chang'd my own opinion of her.

Capt. What you have found her out yourself, Sir?

Tor. Yes, he has made a trifling discovery.

Gen. S'death, don't make me contemptible to my son. *(aside to* Tor.

Capt. But, Sir, what instance of her precious behaviour has come to your knowledge? For an hour has scarcely elapsed, since you thought her a miracle of goodness

Tor. Ay, he has thought her a miracle of goodness, within this quarter of an hour.

Gen. Why she has a manner that wou'd impose upon all the world.

Capt. Yes, but she has a manner also to undeceive the world thoroughly.

Tor. That we have found pretty recently; however, in this land of liberty, none are to be pronounced guilty, 'till they are positively convicted; I can't therefore find against Miss Walsingham, upon the bare strength of presumptive evidence.

Capt. Presumptive evidence! hav'n't I promis'd you ocular demonstration?

Tor. Ay, but 'till we receive this demonstration, my good friend, we cannot give judgement.

Capt. Then I'll tell you at once, who is the object of her honourable affections.

Gen. Who— who—

Capt. What would you think if they were plac'd on Belville?

Gen. Upon Belville! has she deserted to him from the corps of virtue?

Capt. Yes, she wrote to him, desiring to be taken from the masquerade to some convenient scene of privacy, and tho' I have seen the letter, she has the impudence to deny her own hand.

Gen. What a fiend is there then disguis'd under the uniform of an angel! Tor.

Tor. The delicate creature that was dying with confusion!

Capt. Only come with me to the masquerade, and you shall see Belville carry her off: 'Twas about the scandalous appointment with him, I was speaking, when you concciv'd I treated her so rudely.

Gen. And you were only anxious to shew her in her real character to me, when I was so exceedingly offended with you.

Capt. Nothing else in the world, Sir; I knew you would despise and detest her, the moment you were acquainted with her baseness.

Gen. How she brazen'd it out before my face, and what a regard she affected for your interest! I was a madman not to listen then to your explanation.

Tor. Tho' you both talk this point well, I still see nothing but strong presumption against Miss Walsingham: Mistakes have already happened, mistakes may happen again; and I will not give up a lady's honour, upon an evidence that wou'd not cast a common pick-pocket at the Old Baily.

Capt. Come to the masquerade then and be convinc'd.

Gen. Let us detach a party for dresses immediately. Yet remember, Torrington, that the punctuality of evidence which is necessary in a court of law, is by no means requisite in a court of honour.

Tor. Perhaps it would be more to the honour of your honourable courts if it was. [*Exeunt.*

The Scene changes to an Apartment at Mrs. Crayon's.

Bel. (*behind.*) My dear, you must excuse me.

Maid. Indeed, Sir, you must not go up stairs.

Bel. Indeed but I will; the man is positive to the house, and I'll search every room in it, from the cellar to the garret, if I don't find the lady. James, don't stir from the street door.

Enter Belville *followed by a Maid.*

Maid. Sir, you are the strangest gentleman I ever met

met with in all my born days:—I wish my mistress was at home.

BEL. I am a strange fellow, my dear—But if your mistress was at home, I shou'd take the liberty of peeping into the apartments.

MAID. Sir, there's company in that room, you can't go in there.

BEL. Now that's the very reason I will go in.

MAID. This must be some great man, or he wou'dn't behave so obstropolous.

BEL. Good manners by your leave a little. *(forcing the door.)* Whoever my gentleman is, I'll call him to a severe reckoning:—I have been just call'd to one myself, for making free with another man's sister.

Enter Leeson *followed by* Connolly.

LEES. Who is it that dares commit an outrage upon this apartment?

CON. An Englishman's very lodging; ay, and an Irishman's too, I hope, is his castle;—an Irishman is an Englishman all the world over.

BEL. Mr. Leeson!

MAID. O we shall have murder. *(running off.)*

CON. Run into that room, my dear, and stay with the young lady. *(Exit Maid.)*

LEES. And Connolly let nobody else into that room.

CON. Let me alone for that, honey, if this gentleman has fifty people.

LEES. Whence is it, Mr. Belville, that you persecute me thus with injuries?

BEL. I am fill'd with astonishment!

CON. Faith, to speak the truth, you do look a little surpriz'd.

LEES. Answer me, Sir; what is the foundation of this new violence?

BEL. I am come, Mr. Leeson, upon an affair, Sir—

CON. The devil burn me if he was half so much confounded a while ago, when there was a naked sword at his breast.

BEL.

Bel. I am come, Mr. Leeſon, upon an affair, Sir, that----How the devil ſhall I open it to him, ſince the tables are ſo fairly turn'd upon me.

Lees. Diſpatch, Sir, for I have company in the next room.

Bel. A lady, I ſuppoſe?

Lees. Suppoſe it is, Sir?

Bel. And the lady's name is Moreland, isn't it, Sir?

Lees. I can't ſee what buſineſs you have with her name, Sir, You took away my ſiſter, and I hope you have no deſigns upon the lady in the next room.

Bel. Indeed but I have.

Lees. The devil you have!

Con. Well, this is the moſt unaccountable man I ever heard of, he'll have all the women in the town, I believe.

Lees, And pray, Sir, what pretenſions, have you to the lady in the next room, even ſuppoſing her to be Miſs Moreland?

Bel. No other pretenſions than what a brother ſhould have to the defence of his ſiſter's honour: You thought yourſelf authoriſed to cut my throat a-while ago in a ſimilar buſineſs.

Lees. And is Miſs Moreland your ſiſter?

Bel. Sir, there is inſolence in that queſtion; you know ſhe is.

Lees. By heaven, I did not know it till this moment; but I rejoice at the diſcovery: This is blow for blow!

Con. Devil burn me but they have fairly made a ſwop of it.

Bel. And you really didn't know that Miſs Moreland was my ſiſter?

Lees. I don't conceive myſelf under much neceſſity of apologizing to you, Sir; but I am incapable of a diſhonourable deſign upon any woman; and tho' Miſs Moreland in our ſhort acquaintance, re-

peatedly

peatedly mentioned her brother, she never once told me that his name was Belville.

Con. And he has had such few opportunities of being in her company, unless by letters, honey, that he knew nothing more of her connections, than her being a sweet pretty creter, and having 30,000 l.

Bel. The fortune, I dare say, no way lessened the force of her attractions.

Lees. I am above dissimulation---It really did not.

Bel. Well, Mr. Leeson, our families have shewn such a very strong inclination to come together, that it would really be a pity to disappoint them.

Con. Upon my soul and so it would; though the dread of being forc'd to have a husband, the young lady tells us, quicken'd her resolution to marry this gentleman.

Bel. O she had no violence of that kind to apprehend from her family; therefore, Mr. Leeson, since you seem as necessary for the girl's happiness, as she seems for your's, you shall marry her here in town, with the consent of all her friends, and save yourself the trouble of an expedition to Scotland.

Lees. Can I believe you serious?

Bel. Zounds, Leeson, that air of surprise is a sad reproach! I didn't surprise you when I did a bad action, but I raise your astonishment, when I do a good one.

Con. And by my soul, Mr. Belville, if you knew how a good action becomes a man, you'd never do a bad one as long as you liv'd.

Lees. You have given me life and happiness in one day, Mr. Belville! however, it is now time you should see your sister; I know you'll be gentle with her, tho' you have so much reason to condemn her choice, and generously remember that her elopement proceeded from the great improbability there was of a beggar's ever meeting with the approbation of her family.

Bel.

BEL. Don't apologize for your circumſtances, Leeſon; a princeſs could do no more than make you happy, and if you make her ſo, you meet her upon terms of the moſt perfect equality.

LEES. This is a new way of thinking, Mr. Belville.

BEL. 'Tis only an honeſt way of thinking, and I conſider my ſiſter a gainer upon the occaſion; for a man of your merit is more difficult to be found, than a woman of her fortune. [*Exeunt Leeſon and Belville.*

CON. What's the reaſon now that I can't ſkip, and laugh, and rejoice, at this affair? Upon my ſoul my heart's as full as if I had met with ſome great misfortune. Well, pleaſure in the extreme is certainly a very painful thing: I am really aſham'd of theſe womans drops, and yet I don't know but that I ought to bluſh for being aſham'd of them, for I am ſure nobody's eye ever looks half ſo well, as when it is disfigured by a tear of humanity. [*Exit.*

ACT V.

SCENE *a Drawing-Room.*

Enter BELVILLE.

BEL. WELL, happineſs is once more mine, and the women are all going in tip-top ſpirits to the maſquerade. Now, Mr. Belville, let me have a few words with you; Miſs Walſingham, the ripe, the luxurious Miſs Walſingham, expects to find you there burning with impatience:----But, my dear friend, after the occurrences of the day, can you be weak enough to plunge into freſh crimes? Can you be baſe
enough

enough to abuse the goodness of that angel your wife; and wicked enough, not only to destroy the innocence which is shelter'd beneath your own roof, but to expose your family perhaps again, to the danger of losing a son, a brother, a father, and a husband? The possession of the three Graces is surely too poor a recompence for the folly you must commit, for the shame you must feel, and the consequences you must hazard. Upon my soul if I struggle a little longer, I shall rise in my own opinion, and be less a rascal than I think myself :---Ay, but the object is bewitching;---the matter will be an eternal secret—and if it is known that I sneak in this pitiful manner from a fine woman, when the whole elysium of her person solicits me :---well, and am I afraid the world should know that I have shrunk from an infamous action?—A thousand blessings on you dear conscience for that one argument;---I shall be an honest man after all—Suppose, however, that I give her the meeting; that's dangerous;--that's dangerous:--and I am so little accustomed to do what is right, that I shall certainly do what is wrong, the moment I am in the way of temptation. Come, Belville, your resolution is not so very slender a dependance, and you owe Miss Walsingham reparation for the injury which you have done her principles. I'll give her the meeting—I'll take her to the house I intended—I'll!----Zounds! what a fool I have been all this time, to look for precarious satisfaction in vice, when there is such exquisite pleasure to be found at a certainty in virtue! [*Exit*

Enter Lady Rachel *and Mrs* Belville.

Lady RACH. For mirth sake don't let him see us: There has been a warm debate between his passion and his conscience.

Mrs. BEL And the latter is the conqueror, my life for it.

Lady RACH. Dear Mrs. Belville you are the best of women, and ought to have the best of husbands.

Mrs. BEL. I *have* the best of husbands.

Lady RACH. I have not time to dispute the matter with you now; but I shall put you into my comedy to teach wives, that the best receipt for matrimonial happiness, is to be deaf, dumb, and blind.

Mrs. BEL. Poh! poh! you are a satirest, Lady Rachel—But we are losing time; shou'dn't we put on our dresses, and prepare for the grand scene?

Lady RACH. Don't you tremble at the trial?

Mrs. BEL. Not in the least, I am sure my heart has no occasion.

Lady RACH. Have you let Miss Walsingham into our little plot?

Mrs. BEL. You know she cou'd not be insensible of Mr. Belville's design upon herself, and it is no farther than that design, we have any thing to carry into execution.

Lady RACH. Well, she may serve to facilitate the matter, and therefore I am not sorry that you have trusted her.

Mrs. BEL. We shall be too late, and then what signifies all your fine plotting.

Lady RACH. Is it not a little pang of jealousy that wou'd fain now quicken our motions?

Mrs. BEL. No, Lady Rachel, it is a certainty of my husband's love and generosity, that makes me wish to come to the trial. I wou'd not exchange my confidence in his affections for all the mines of Peru; so nothing you can say will make me miserable.

Lady RACH. You are a most unaccountab'e woman; so away with you. [*Exeunt.*

SCENE *continued.*

Enter Spruce *and* Ghastly.

SPRUCE. Why, Ghastly, the old general your master is a greater fool than I ever thought he was: He want to marry Miss Walsingham?

GHAST. Mrs. Tempest suspected that there was some-

something going forward, by all his hugger-mugger consulting with Mr. Torrington; and so set me on to listen.

SPRUCE. She's a good friend of your's, and that thing she made the General give you the other day in the hospital, is I suppose a snug hundred a year.

GHAST. Better than two; I wash for near four thousand people: there was a major of horse who put in for it, and pleaded a large family—

SPRUCE. With long services, I suppose.

GHAST. Yes, but Mrs. Tempest insisted upon my long services; so the major was set aside—However to keep the thing from the damn'd News-papers, I fancy he will succeed the barber, who died last night, poor woman, of a lying-in fever, after being brought to bed of three children.—Places in public institutions.—

SPRUCE. Are often sweetly dispos'd I think of asking Belville for something, one of these days.

GHAST. He has great interest.

SPRUCE. I might be a justice of peace, if I pleas'd, and in a shabby neighbourhood, where the mere swearing would bring in something tolerable; but there are so many strange people let into the commission now-a-days, that I shou'dn't like to have my name in the list.

GHAST. You are right.

SPRUCE. No, no, I leave that to paltry tradesmen, and shall think of some little sinecure, or a small pension on the Irish establishment.

GHAST. Well, success attend you. I must hobble home as fast as I can, to know if Mrs. Tempest has any orders. O, there's a rare storm brewing for our old goat of a General.

SPRUCE. When shall we crack a bottle together?

GHAST. O, I shan't touch a glass of Claret these three weeks; for last night I gave nature a little fillip, with a drunken bout, according to the doctor's directions; I have entirely left off bread, and I am in great hopes that I shall get rid of my gout by these means,

espe-specially if I can learn to eat my meat quite raw like a cannibal.

SPRUCE. Ha, ha, ha!

GHAST. Look at me, Spruce, I was once as likely a young fellow as any under ground in the whole parish of St. James's:--but waiting on the General so many years.

SPRUCE. Ay, and following his example, Ghastly.

GHAST. 'Tis too true: has reduc'd me to what you see. These miserable spindles wou'd do very well for a lord or a duke, Spruce; but they are a sad disgrace to a poor valet de chambre. [*Exit.*

SPRUCE. Well, I don't believe there's a gentleman's gentleman within the weekly bills, who joins a prudent solicitude for the main-chance, to a strict care of his constitution, better than myself. I have a little girl who stands me in about three guineas a week; I never bet more than a pound upon a rubber of whist; I always sleep with my head very warm; and swallow a new laid egg every morning with my chocolate. [*Exit.*

The Scene changes to the Street, two Chairs cross the Stage, knock at a Door, and set down BELVILLE *and a Lady.*

BEL. This way, my dear creature! [*Exeunt.*

Enter Gen. Savage, *Capt.* Savage, *and* Torrington.

CAPT. There!. there they go in:----You see the place is quite convenient, not twenty yards from the masquerade.

GEN. How closely the fellow sticks to her.

TOR. Like the great seal to the peerage patent of a chancellor. But, gentlemen, we have still no more than proof presumptive:---where is the ocular demonstration which we were to have?

CAPT. I'll swear to the blue domino; 'tis a very remarkable one, and so is Belville's.

TOR. You wou'd have rare custom among the New-
gate

gate follicitors, if you'd venture an oath upon the identity of the party under it.

GEN. 'Tis the very fize and fhape of Mifs Walfingham.

TOR. And yet I have a ftrange notion that there is a trifling *alibi* in this cafe.

GEN. It wou'd be a damn'd affair if we fhou'd be countermin'd.

CAPT. O, follow me, here's the door left luckily open, and I'll foon clear up the matter beyond a queftion. [*Enters the houfe.*

TOR. Why your fon is mad, General. This muft produce a deadly breach with Belville. For heav'n's fake, let's go in and prevent any exceffes of his rafhnefs.

GEN. By all means, or the poor fellow's generous anxiety on my account may be productive of very fatal confequences. *Exeunt.*

The Scene changes to an apartment, Belville *unmafked, and a lady in a blue domino mafk'd.*

BEL. My dear Mifs Walfingham, we are now perfectly fafe, yet I will by no means intreat you to unmafk, becaufe I am convinc'd, from the propriety with which you repuls'd my addreffes this morning, that you intend the prefent interview fhould make me ftill more deeply fenfible of my prefumption.----I never lied fo aukwardly in all my life; if it was to make her comply, I fhould be at no lofs for language. (*afide*) The fituation in which I muft appear before you, Madam, is certainly a very humiliating one; but I am perfuaded that your generofity will be gratified to hear, that I have bid an everlafting adieu to my profligacy, and am now only alive to the virtues of Mrs. Belville.----She won't fpeak—I don't wonder at it, for brazen as I am myfelf, if I met fo mortifying a rejection, I fhould be curfedly out of countenance.

(*afide.*
CAPT.

CAPT. *(behind)* I will go in.
GEN. *(behind.)* I command you to desist.
TOR. *(behind.)* This will be an affair for the Old-Bailey.

(The noise grows more violent, and continues.

BEL. Why, what the devil is all this?—Don't be alarm'd, Miss Walsingham, be assur'd I'll protect you at the hazard of my life;—step into this closet,—you shan't be discover'd depend upon it; *(she goes in)*: And now to find out the cause of this confusion. *(unlocks the door.*

Enter Gen. Savage, *Capt.* Savage, *and* Torrington.

BEL. Savage! what is the meaning of this strange behaviour?

CAPT. Where is Miss Walsingham?

BEL. So then, Sir, this is a premeditated scheme, for which I am oblig'd to your friendship.

CAPT. Where's Miss Walsingham, Sir?

GEN. Dear Belville, he is out of his senses; this storm was entirely against my orders.

TOR. If he proceeds much longer in these vagaries, we must amuse him with a commission of lunacy.

BEL. This is neither a time nor a place for argument, Mr. Torrington; but as you and the General seem to be in the possession of your senses, I shall be glad if you'll take this very friendly gentleman away; and depend upon it, I shan't die in his debt for the present obligation.

CAPT. And depend upon it, Sir, pay the obligation when you will, I shan't stir 'till I see Miss Walsingham.—Look'ee, Belville, there are secret reasons for my behaving in this manner; reasons, which you yourself will approve, when you know them;—my father here—

GEN. Disavows your conduct in every particular, and would rejoice to see you at the halberds.

TOR

Tor. And, for my part, I told him previously 'twas a downright burglary.

Bel. Well, gentlemen, let your different motives for breaking in upon me in this agreeable manner, be what they may, I don't see that I am less annoy'd by my friends than my enemy. I must therefore again, request that you will all walk down stairs.

Capt. I'll first walk into this room.

Bel. Really, I think you will not.

Gen. What phrenzy possesses the fellow to urge this matter farther?

Capt. While there's a single doubt she triumphs over justice; *(drawing.)* I will go into that room.

Bel. Then you must make your way thro' me.

Enter Mrs. Belville.

Mrs. Bel. Ah!

Capt. There, I knew she was in the room:—there's the blue domino.

Gen. Put up your sword, if you don't desire to be cashier'd from my favour for ever.

Bel. Why, wou'd you come out, madam? But, you have nothing to apprehend.

Capt. Pray, madam, will you have the goodness to unmask?

Bel. She shan't unmask.

Capt. I say she shall.

Bel. I say she shall not.

Mrs. Bel. Pray, let me oblige the gentleman?

Capt. Death and destruction, here's a discovery!

Gen. *and* Tor. Mrs. Belville!

Mrs. Bel. Yes, Mrs. Belville, gentlemen: Is confugal fidelity so very terrible a thing now a-days, that a man is to suffer death for being found in company with his own wife?

Bel. My love, this is a surprize, indeed—But it is a most agreeable one; since you find me really asham'd of my former follies, and cannot now doubt the sincerity of my reformation. *Mrs.* Bel

Mrs. Bel. I am too happy! this single moment wou'd over pay a whole life of anxiety.

Bel. Where shall I attend you? Will you return to the masquerade?

Mrs. Bel. O no! Lady Rachel and Miss Walsingham are by this time at our house, with Mr. Leeson and the Irish gentleman whom you press'd into our party, impatiently expecting the result of this adventure.

Bel. Give me leave to conduct you home then from this scene of confusion. To-morrow, Captain Savage, I shall beg the favour of your explanation; *(aside to him as he goes out.)* Kind gentlemen, your most humble servant.

Mrs. Bel. And when you next disturb a *tête à tête*, for pity to a poor wife, don't let it be so very uncustomary a party, as the matrimonial one.

(*Exeunt* Bel. *and Mrs.* Bel.

Gen. *(to the Capt.)* So, Sir, you have led us upon a blessed expedition here.

Tor. Now, don't you think that if your courts of honour, like our courts of law, search'd a little minutely into evidence, it wou'd be equally to the credit of their understandings?

Capt. Tho' I am cover'd with confusion at my mistake (for you see, Belville was mistaken as well as myself,) I am overjoy'd at this discovery of Miss Walsingham's innocence.

Gen. I shou'd exult in it too, with a *feu de joy*, if it didn't now shew the impossibility of her ever being Mrs. Savage.

Capt. Dear Sir, why should you think that an impossibility? Tho' some mistakes have occurr'd in consequence I suppose, of Mrs. Belville's little plot upon her husband, I dare say Miss Walsingham may yet be prevail'd upon to come into our family.

Tor. Take care of a new error in your proceedings, young gentleman.

Gen.

GEN. Ay, another defeat would make us compleatly despicable.

CAPT. Sir, I'll forfeit my life, if she does not consent to the marriage this very night.

GEN. Only bring this matter to bear, and I'll forgive you every thing.

TOR. The Captain shou'd be inform'd, I think General, that she declin'd it peremptorily this evening.

GEN. Ay, do you hear that, Horace?

CAPT. I am not at all surpriz'd at it, considering the general misconception we labour'd under. But I'll immediately to Belville's, explain the whole mystery, and conclude every thing to your satisfaction. [*Exit.*

GEN. So, Torrington, we shall be able to take the field again, you see.

TOR. But how in the name of wonder has your son found out your intention of marrying Miss Walsingham? I look'd upon myself as the only person acquainted with the secret.

GEN. That thought has march'd itself two or three times to my own recollection. For tho' I gave him some distant hints of the affair, I took particular care to keep behind the works of a proper circumspection.

TOR. O, if you gave him any hints at all, I am not surpriz'd at his discovering every thing.

GEN. I shall be all impatience 'till I hear of his interview with Miss Walsingham: Suppose my dear friend we went to Belville's, 'tis but in the next street, and we shall be there in the lighting of a match.

TOR. Really this is a pretty business for a man of my age and profession, trot here, trot there. But, as I have been weak enough to make myself a kind of party in the cause, I own that I have curiosity enough to be anxious about the determination.

GEN. Come along my old boy; and remember the song, " *Servile spirits*, &c." [*Exeunt.*

The Scene changes to Belville's.

Enter Captain Savage *and Miss* Walsingham.

CAPT. Nay, but my dearest Miss Walsingham, the extenuation of my own conduct to Belville made it absolutely necessary for me to discover my engagements with you; and as happiness is now so fortunately in our reach, I flatter myself you will be prevail'd upon to forgive an error, which proceeded only from an extravagance of love.

Miss WAL. To think me capable of such an action, Captain Savage! I am terrified at the idea of a union with you, and it is better for a woman at any time, to sacrifice an insolent lover, than to accept of a suspicious husband.

CAPT. In the happiest unions, my dearest creature, there must be always something to overlook on both sides.

Miss WAL. Very civil, truly.

CAPT. Pardon me, my life, for this frankness; and recollect, that if the lover has thro' misconception been unhappily guilty, he brings a husband altogether reform'd to your hands.

Miss WAL. Well, I see I must forgive you at last, so I may as well make a merit of necessity, you provoking creature.

CAPT. And may I hope, indeed, for the blessing of this hand?

Miss WAL. Why, you wretch, would you have me force it upon you? I think, after what I have said, a soldier might have ventur'd to take it without farther ceremony.

CAPT. Angelic creature! thus I seize it as my lawful prize.

Miss WAL. Well, but now you have obtained this inestimable prize, Captain, give me again leave to ask if you have had a certain explanation with the General?

CAPT.

CAPT. How can you doubt it?

Miss WAL. And he is really impatient for our marriage?

CAPT. 'Tis incredible how earnest he is.

Miss WAL. What, did he tell you of his Interview with me this evening, when he brought Mr. Torrington?

CAPT. He did.

Miss WAL. O, then, I can have do doubt.

CAPT. If a shadow of doubt remains, here he comes to remove it. Joy, my dear Sir! joy a thousand times!

Enter General Savage, *and* Torrington.

GEN. What, my dear boy, have you carried the day?

Miss WAL. I have been weak enough to indulge him with a victory, indeed, General.

GEN. *None but the brave, none but the brave, &c.*
[Singing.

TOR. I congratulate you heartily on this decree, General.

GEN. This had nearly proved a day of disappointment, but the stars have fortunately turn'd it in my favour, and now I reap the rich reward of my victory. *(Salutes her)*

CAPT. And here I take her from you, as the greatest good which heav'n can send me.

Miss WAL. O, Captain!

GEN. You take her as the greatest good which heav'n can send you, sirrah; I take her as the greatest good which heav'n can send me: And now what have you to say to her?

Miss WAL. General Savage!

TOR. Here will be a fresh injunction to stop proceedings.

Miss WAL. Are we never to have done with mistakes?

GEN. What mistakes can have happen'd now my sweetest? you deliver'd up your dear hand to me this moment?

Miss WAL. True, Sir; but I thought you were going to bestow my dear hand upon this dear gentleman.

GEN. How! that dear gentleman!

CAPT. I am thunder-struck!

TOR. General----*None but the brave, &c.* [*sings.*

GEN. So the covert way is clear'd at last; and you have imagin'd that I was all along negociating for this fellow, when I was gravely soliciting for myself?

Miss WAL. No other idea, Sir, ever once enter'd my imagination.

TOR. General.----*Noble minds should ne'er despair, &c.* [*sings.*

GEN. Zounds! here's all the company pouring upon us in full gallop, and I shall be the laughing stock of the whole town.

Enter Belville, *Mrs.* Belville, *Lady* Rachel, Leeson *and* Connolly.

BEL. Well, General, we have left you a long time together. Shall I give you joy?

GEN. No; wish me demolish'd in the fortifications of Dunkirk.

Mrs. BEL. What's the matter?

Lady RACH. The General appears disconcerted.

LEES. The gentleman looks as if he had fought a hard battle.

CON. Ay, and gain'd nothing but a defeat, my dear.

TOR. I'll shew cause for his behaviour.

GEN. Death and damnation! not for the world. I am taken by surprise here; let me consider a moment how to cut my way thro' the enemy.

Miss Wal. How cou'd you be deceiv'd in this manner. *(To Capt.*

Lady Rach. O, Mr. Torrington, we are much oblig'd to you; you have been in town ever since last night, and only see us now by accident.

Tor. I have been very busy, Madam; but you look sadly, very sadly indeed! your old disorder the jaundice, I suppose, has been very troublesome to you?

Lady Rach. Sir, you have a very extraordinary mode of complimenting your acquaintance.

Con. I don't believe for all that, that there's a word of a lie in the truth he speaks. *(aside*

Mrs. Bel. Miss Walsingham, Capt. Savage has been telling Mr. Belville and me of a very extraordinary mistake.

Miss Wal. 'Tis very strange indeed, mistake on mistake.

Bel. 'Tis no way strange to find every body properly struck with the merit of Miss Walsingham.

Miss Wal. A compliment from you now, Mr. Belville, is really worth accepting.

Gen. If I thought the affair cou'd be kept a secret, by making the town over to my son, since I am utterly shut out myself----

Capt. He seems exceedingly embarrassed.

Gen. If I thought that;---why mortified as I must be in giving it up, I think I cou'd resolve upon the manœuvre, to save myself from universal ridicule: but it can't be;---it can't be; and I only double my own disappointment in rewarding the disobedience of the rascal who has supplanted me. There!---there! they are all talking of it, all laughing at me, and I shall run mad!

Mrs. Temp. *(behind)* I say, you feather-headed puppy, he is in this house; my own servant saw him come in, and I will not stir 'till I find him.

Gen.

GEN. She here!---then deliberation is over, and I am entirely blown up.

Lady RACH. I'll take notes of this affair.

Enter Mrs. Tempeſt,

Mrs. TEMP. Mighty well, Sir, So you are in love it ſeems;---and you want to be married it ſeems?

LEES. My bleſſed aunt!---O how proud I am of the relation.

GEN. Dear Bab, give me quarter before all this company.

Mrs. TEMP. You are in love, you old fool, are you? and you want to marry Miſs Walſingham, indeed!

CON. I never heard a pleaſanter ſpoken gentlewoman---O hone, if I had the taming of her, ſhe ſhou'd never be abuſive, without keeping a civil tongue in her head.

Mrs. TEM. Well, Sir, and when is the happy day to be fix'd?

BEL. What the devil, is this true, General?

GEN. True.---Can you believe ſuch an abſurdity?

Mrs. TEMP. Why, will you deny, you miſerable old mummy, that you made propoſal of marriage to her?---

GEN. Yes I do---no I don't---propoſals of marriage!

Miſs WAL. In favour of your ſon.---I'll help him out a little. [*aſide*

GEN. Yes, in favour of my ſon---what the devil ſhall I do?

Mrs. BEL. Shall I take a leſſon from this lady, Mr. Belville? Perhaps if the women of virtue were to pluck up a little ſpirit, they might be ſoon as well treated as kept miſtreſſes.

Mrs. TEMP. Harkee, General Savage, I believe you aſſert a falſehood; but if you ſpeak the truth, give your ſon this moment to Miſs Walſingham, and let me be fairly rid of my rival.

GEN. My ſon! Miſs Walſingham!---Miſs Walſingham, my ſon!

BEL.

BEL. It will do, Horace; it will do.

Mrs. TEMP. No prevarications, General Savage; do what I bid you inftantly, or by all the wrongs of an enraged woman, I'll fo expofe you.——

CON. What a fine fellow this is, to have the command of an army!

GEN. If Mifs Walfingham can be prevailed upon.

TOR. O, fhe'll oblige you readily---But you muft fettle a good fortune upon your fon.

Mrs. TEMP. That he fhall do.

Mrs. BEL. Mifs Walfingham, my Dear---

Mifs WAL. I can refufe nothing either to your requeft, or to the requeft of the General.

GEN. Oblige me with your hand then, Madam: come here you——come here Captain. There, there is Mifs Walfingham's hand for you.

CON. And as pretty a little fift it is, as any in the three kingdoms.

GEN. Torrington fhall fettle the fortune.

LEES. I give you joy moft heartily, Madam.

BEL. We all give her joy.

CAPT. Mine is beyond the power of expreffion.

Mifs WAL. *(afide to the company)* And fo is the General's, I believe.

CON. O faith, that may be eafily feen by the fweetnefs of his countenance.

TOR. Well, the caufe being now at laft determin'd, I think we may all retire from the court.

GEN. And without any great credit, I fear, to the General.

CON. By my foul, you may fay that.——

Mrs. TEMP. Do you murmur, Sir?---Come this moment home with me.

GEN. I'll go any where to hide this miferable head of mine: what a damn'd campaign have I made of it!

[*Exeunt Gen. and Mrs. Temp.*

CON.

88 The SCHOOL for WIVES.

Con. Upon my soul, if I was in the General's place, I'd divide the house with this devil; I'd keep within doors myself, and make her take the outside.

Bel. The day has been a busy one, thanks to the communicative disposition of the Captain.

Mrs. Bel. And the evening should be chearful.

Bel. I shan't therefore part with one of you, 'till we have had a hearty laugh at our general adventures.

Miss Wal. They have been very whimsical indeed; yet if represented on the stage, I hope they wou'd be found not only entertaining, but instructive.

Lady Rach. Instructive! why the modern Critics say that the only business of Comedy is to make people laugh.

Bel. That is degrading the dignity of letters exceedingly, as well as lessening the utility of the stage ---A good comedy is a capital effort of genius, and should therefore be directed to the noblest purposes.

Miss Wal. Very true; and unless we learn something while we chuckle, the carpenter who nails a Pantomime together, will be entitled to more applause, than the best comic poet in the kingdom.

[*Exeunt omnes.*

FINIS.

www.ingramcontent.com/pod-product-compliance
Lightning Source LLC
Chambersburg PA
CBHW030411170426
43202CB00010B/1570